THE NOMAD'S GUIDE TO
TAKING YOUR DOG ON THE ROAD
IN AUSTRALIA
AF604991

THE NOMAD'S GUIDE TO

TAKING YOUR DOG ON THE ROAD IN AUSTRALIA

Paul Chai

Contents

INTRODUCTION

Dog, gone: why take your pooch on the road?

The thing about being part of a pack is that members of the pack do everything together – and that includes hitting the road. For many pet owners, a key benefit of owning a dog is that they are more easily portable than other pets, and your canine companion can be buckled into the back seat for short trips or long ones, beach walks or forest hikes.

Travelling with a dog adds a different dimension to a driving holiday. You stop more, take more time and often discover things you would not normally see when you are whizzing past on the freeway; road tripping with your dog allows you to quite literally stop and smell the roses, the grass, the trees or anything else that has an appealing scent.

Neil Mackay, president of the Old English Sheepdog Club of Victoria has owned the large, shaggy breed for over 30 years, and he takes his pets with him when he goes on holidays.

'Travelling with a dog is everything you want from a dog, it's companionship, it's unconditional love, you try to take them to as many places as you can because that's your family,' Mackay says.

'When I had my first Old English sheepdog back in the 80s I would travel for obedience trials. It was harder back then but today we are much more user-friendly and we can take dogs to cafes and restaurants.'

Now, Mackay travels with his two-year-old Old English sheepdog, Angus, in full Dulux-dog coat, and takes him with him wherever he can. He believes people should be aware that when they have a dog, they become that animal's whole world; not in an abstract sense, but in the real sense that you are the gatekeeper to their social interactions, their exercise, their food and their travel.

'While kids grow up and become independent, dogs don't. They rely on you for life,' Mackay adds. 'To be cared for, to be protected, to be socialised, and if you don't do it you let the dog down. You treat them like you want to be treated.'

So it makes sense that they get to holiday with you.

Holidays but not as you know them

Australia has one of the highest dog-ownership rates in the world. The RSPCA notes that 61 per cent of Australian households own a pet of some kind with 40 per cent of them being home to a dog, and that was before COVID-19 made dogs seriously hot property. The organisation also discovered that during lockdown there was a 45 per cent surge in dog adoptions, and puppies were fetching thousands of dollars above their pre-COVID asking price.

A main reason for the adoption of a pet is companionship, and for many pet owners taking their beloved pet on a trip is like taking their child. But you have to accept that your holidays, like the rest of your life, are in for some drastic change. The biggest change is how much planning must go into a holiday. With your dog in the back seat your accommodation options shrink – a lot.

Despite our high rates of dog ownership, and the changes that Neil Mackay has seen since the dog-unfriendly 1980s, Australia can still be pretty resistant to having pets in hotels, cafes and restaurants, primarily due to strict food-hygiene rules. But things are starting to change.

The latest hospitality trend is dog-friendly hotels, high-end places like Ovolo, Elements, Abode and The Langham in Melbourne. The QT hotel chain even has a Head of Treats to prepare food for canine guests.

Dogs have always been a staple of caravan parks, but now you can stay in motels with a designated dog run next to your room, or campgrounds that are dog-friendly right on the cusp of a national park. You can rent cabins, Airbnbs or stay on thousands of acres on outback cattle stations. We are not at the level of Europe yet, where you will see a pooch under every second Parisian cafe table, but with the increase in COVID pets Australia might just be on the cusp of a pet travel revolution.

However, you will need to properly organise your trip, as the spontaneity of just pulling over to a place with a 'vacancy' sign is long gone. You may also need to be more flexible about your travel schedule depending on how your dog travels. You can tell your kids to hold on until the next service station but some dogs, younger ones in particular, may need more stops along the way.

Travelling with a dog means that everywhere you stop you are not only thinking of where to eat and what to see but mentally mapping the local list of dog parks, dog-friendly attractions, and even vets in case of emergency. It's a bit like going back to travelling with a big, furry toddler: it requires patience and preparation but there are also great upsides.

Watching your dog experience new things is a reward in itself. We watched our Old English sheepdog pup, Orinoco, suddenly discover his shepherding gene as he instinctively tried to herd a flock of rescue sheep at a farmstay in Victoria. We swam with him in the beautifully secluded bay of Sirius Cove in Sydney, somewhere my wife had never been despite spending most of her life in the Harbour City. And we found the best view of Canberra from the hilltop of the dog-friendly National Arboretum.

Travelling with your dog may create restrictions, but if you work within them, it offers you a holiday just as rewarding, if not more so, than any break you have ever taken.

Neil Mackay's travel tips

Mackay has spent a lot of time taking his Old English sheepdog, Angus, on the road, and rarely goes away without him.

Have water on hand at all times. Fresh water and a water bowl must travel everywhere with you.

When you are travelling give the dog breaks. 'They say that dogs learn to live in the world by stopping and smelling on their walks,' Mackay says. 'When I walk Angus it is his walk not mine, so if he wants to stop and smell the grass that's fine, it doesn't worry me.'

TRAVEL TAILS

Justin Noonan and Charlie the rescue moodle

Justin Noonan is a storm chaser. What started as a hobby, or 'sport', back in 2001 now sees Noonan paid to report on, follow and photograph some of Australia's wildest weather. And he takes his rescue moodle, Charlie, along for the sometimes-hairy ride.

'I grew up on a farm out near Mt Tamborine and we had a big flood there in 1996 and that was the catalyst for it, then a couple of months later Cyclone Justin came along and decided it wanted to pester the Queensland coast for about three and a half weeks,' Noonan says.

After those two events, Noonan joined the Australian Severe Weather Association and a passion was born. In 2001 he got his driver's licence 'and I had my first chase and I have never looked back.'

'I am a bit of an adrenaline junkie so it fills that void,' he says. 'There is something really special about being out there and seeing all these ingredients, you can't physically see, form one of the greatest creations on the planet, really. You are feeling the wind on your face, the hair stands up on the back of your neck then lightning strikes close or large hail falls and the thunder ... there is just something special about it.'

Noonan nearly lost his life in a US tornado in 2011 in Missouri. The tornado was the highest on the scale with winds of over 250 miles an hour and it was the seventh deadliest tornado in US history.

Noonan's canine storm-chasing companion, Charlie, was a rescue dog who would 'have a go' at everyone who came into the pound, until Noonan turned up for a visit. Then Charlie simply wandered over and hopped in his lap like it was fate. He was quite young so when it came time for Noonan to jump into his hail-ravaged tray-back ute and chase some weird weather, he took Charlie along for the ride.

'There was something about it, he just loved it. He was sitting out in the paddock with us watching the storm develop and every time after that he would see me pick up my camera and tripod and just want to come along,' Noonan says. 'He has been through it all now and he absolutely loves it. We get out there and he loves having the wind blow in his face.'

Funnily enough, if Charlie is at home and he hears thunder and lightning he is scared, just like a normal dog, but out there on a chase it just does not seem to worry him at all. 'It's kind of bizarre really,' Noonan adds.

Charlie rides up front in the passenger seat while Noonan's gear – cameras, microphones, lenses, GoPros, window mounts, tripods – is banished to the back. 'He gets his bed on the front seat and he loves to be able to see out the front, see what is happening and enjoy the show,' he says.

'One of the most interesting things he has seen is large hail, something that I really love. I will try to drive through the biggest hail that I find and 29 October 2020 I was in northern New South Wales and I decided to punch through some cricket-ball hail. That was fun – I lost a windscreen and did a lot of damage to the car but all those dents kind of blend into one these days. We like to call them "trophies".'

Even daredevil dogs need their breaks, so Noonan says he stops every couple of hours on any road trip, he packs extra food because of the unknown nature of their travels and what might happen, and always takes his bed into any accommodation so he can protect the soft furnishings of anywhere he stays.

CHAPTER ONE

BEFORE YOU GO

Proper pup-eration: getting ready for the trip

You know, as a dog owner, that having a pet requires a lot of, well, stuff. There are leads, treats, favourite toys and more, and now they have to be packed up and put in the car or van. So, you need to sit down and make a complete list of what to pack if you are on an extended trip (see more options in the gear section, page 18).

For new doggy travellers a good tip is to start with short trips to see how your dog takes to car travel and life on the road. Some dogs get car sick, some dogs simply don't like driving and need to be desensitised. If you have not taken your dog anywhere, start with short day trips to see how they like life on the road.

You will need to make sure your dog has its own space in the car. Room to curl up but also do a full sleep stretch. The more comfortable your pet is the longer you will be able to drive. A happy dog is a calm and quiet dog.

If your dog is a nervous traveller despite the short test-trips you can try calming sprays like Adaptil, calming chews like Vetalogica's VitaRapid Tranquil Daily Treats or, if your dog is crate trained, drive them tucked up in their safe space with a few handy toys to keep them amused.

You must also make certain that your dog's vaccinations are up to date and check their microchip and the details on any dog tags they might have (you don't want an old phone number on there when you lose your dog in the middle of nowhere). If you don't have a dog collar, get one. It will be well worth it when you think your dog is lost forever and you get a mobile phone call from just a couple of caravans away.

Be prepared to up the treat quotient as your dog will be learning to do a lot of new things and cope with a lot of new situations and stimuli. But make sure you factor these treats into your dog's normal healthy diet. A road trip should not be an excuse for weight gain or poor diet, but like us on holidays, you might have to relax the rules just a bit.

The number one thing to be aware of is to make sure your dog has an easily accessible supply of fresh water or make plenty of stops so they can hydrate. We all know that 'dogs die in hot cars', but they do not need to be parked cars.

You will need to accept that this road trip might get messy. You already know that your dog is happiest when he is crusted in the dirt of a great adventure, but sometimes that adventure is going to happen on a brief stop and you are going to have a dirty dog ready to jump back in the car. You can prepare somewhat by carrying a short hose and a quick-dry towel with you but you will also need to pack a fair bit of acceptance as well.

Put plastic bags in every nook and cranny of the car. A responsible dog owner always picks up after their dog whether at the local dog park or an outback roadhouse. In particular, when you are in far-away spots dog poop can find its way into and pollute local waterways, or simply scare off local wildlife.

Be aware of local wildlife, both good and bad. We all know that 'everything in Australia can kill you' from ticks to tiger snakes, but your dog doesn't know that. He just sees a very exciting, scaly plaything, so make sure your dog is safe and under effective control.

With that in mind, a key question when you are travelling with your dog is: is this place appropriate for them? You can take your dog anywhere, but should you? If your destination is a national park or a place full of other no-go zones your pet will not have a very good time. Equally, if your dog is elderly, has health issues or simply does not like to travel then you should make sure that taking them with you is the best option. Do not limit yourself too much but do make sure you consider the accessibility of the region and the capability of your pet when you decide where you want to travel and if your dog should come with you.

But once you have made the decision you can then take a deep breath and a deep dive with our advice on what you need to know and what you need to take with you, so you don't look back when you head off into the highway sunset with your dog's tongue flapping excitedly in the breeze.

TRAVEL TAILS

Leonie and Geoff Sargood, and Sammy the cavoodle

Leonie Sargood spent two years on the road in a caravan with Sammy and her husband Geoff, taking the pooch all over Australia. 'I just love seeing his excitement at seeing new places,' Sargood says. 'Sammy is such a social dog. I love his company, his is just so enthused about going to new places and meeting new people, pretty much like humans.'

Throughout the two years of travelling, Sargood was surprised at just how accepting people were about having their dog in cafes, restaurants, and even shops ('We asked first, of course!').

'We travelled for three and half months in Tassie and not once were we refused,' Sargood says. 'And caravan parks are much more dog-friendly than they used to be. I would say it has changed a lot in the past five years.'

If they did need to go anywhere without Sammy, Sargood says they would always find someone willing to help where they were staying. 'The owners of caravan parks usually know someone locally that will take your dog,' Sargood says. 'We stayed at the Fraser Coast and because there is whale watching there we found the caravan park had a list of people that would take care of your dog if you wanted to head out for the day.'

Sargood believes that one of the big bonuses of travelling with a dog is that it creates a greater sense of community.

'In a caravan park we are stopped all the time when walking the dog,' Sargood says. 'It absolutely improves your communication with others that are camping or caravanning with dogs. People are interested in your story and what you have done. It increases your contact with people from all walks of life.'

Her top tip is to make sure your dog is comfortable when it travels so you are happier on the trip and less stressed on arrival. For Sammy that meant a booster seat so that he could watch the world go by.

Pack mentality: all the gear you need

What you pack and what you need will depend on your lifestyle, your dog, your trip and the length, but there are some things that we all need on a pet-friendly road trip.

We will never get sick of saying plenty of food and water, but when it comes to the rest of the gear we have compiled an exhaustive list of what you will need for your car-bound canine.

This is not just a list for a quick weekend, or even week away, but a comprehensive look at the gear and gadgets that might make travelling on tar just that little bit easier.

The weekender basics

Vaccination papers

This is like a dog passport if you want to get some on-the-road doggy daycare or even just see a vet. Make sure you have this with you and take a photo of it and store it on your phone as well. Have it in as many places as you can. If you have pet insurance it does not generally need to change when you travel, as there is not really pet travel insurance on offer in Australia unless you transport your dog overseas. Just check with your provider to make sure everything is up to date and find out what you need to do to make a claim while you're away from home.

Dog poop bags

This should probably be number one, but make sure you take far more than you think you need. And in the spirit of being out in nature, consider the sustainability of your poo bags and try a brand like Rufus & Coco that makes the Do Good Poo Bags that are biodegradable and made out of corn starch; rufusandcoco.com.au.

Grooming equipment

If you think you do a lot of grooming at home, wait for all the burrs, dirt and dust that the wide-open road offers. Make sure you have all the combs, clippers and scissors that you need to keep your pooch perfect. If you are travelling in a van you should also consider a hair dryer for your dog as they are going to get wet, a lot.

Dog bed

Whether your pet likes to sleep on a rug, a pillow, or a posh, plush offering you need to pack something for them to chill on. If it still has the smell of home on it for the first leg of the trip that is a good thing.

Crate or kennel

If your dog is crate trained you will get a better night's sleep by keeping up the routine. The You & Me brand available at Petbarn do a great soft crate that will easily fit in most car boots, as well as a canvas play pen suitable for all bar the largest of dogs; petbarn.com.au.

Leads, collars and harnesses

You will need your usual walking equipment, but also a travel harness that clips into the seatbelt. The EzyDog travel harness provides plenty of support in the event of a bit of a bingle and is teamed with the car restraint that clips your dog in safely; ezydog.com.au.

Medication

Keep a supply of flea and tick medication and wormers, but for a full safety guide see our section on dog first-aid kits on page 42.

Favourite toys

With all this new excitement your dog is going to require some soothing, or some distraction, so be sure you have their favourite sleep toy if they have one. For breaks you need to have a ball or frisbee to hand so you can help to wear them out – a tired dog is much more likely to be happy to get back into the car.

Towels

Plenty. For the back seat, for towelling off your dog, or for any doggy accidents.

The mega-pack for a long haul

Fencing

If you are planning on some long-distance van travel you might want to invest in some pet fencing so you can confine your dog with an enclosure that can encircle your van or car. Bunnings sells the RapidMesh eight-panel animal enclosure; bunnings.com.au.

Also travel with a bag of snap clips that can hold the fencing in a variety of shapes as well as hold a roll of poo bags to a lead and help keep towels off the floor of the van.

Tether lead

If you are staying in the bush you will want to give your dog space but not let them wander too far away. A good idea is a lead with plenty of room to move like the You & Me Super Dog Tie Out Cable that allows 6 metres of roaming room to dogs up to 68 kilograms when paired with a spiral stake that can be driven into the ground; petbarn.com.au.

Make sure your pet is used to having this much rope without getting tangled up. This is not a set-up for puppies.

Light-up collar

Handy for night-time ablutions in the caravan park with low lighting, getting a glowing LED collar may look naff in the suburbs but can be a great idea in the great outdoors. Try the Rufus & Coco version with both flashing and standard LED options; rufusandcoco.com.au.

You might also consider a dog collar GPS tracker for an even better night's sleep.

Small shovel

If you are camping you may choose to use a more natural method of dog poo tidying by burying the waste in a very deep hole. Something like the Gerber Gorge folding shovel from Elite Outdoor Gear should do the trick; eliteoutdoorgear.com.au. A short-handled rake is also useful if you are camping for a while and want to clear an area of debris that will stick to a dog's fur.

Life jacket

If you are planning a seabound adventure, or even just spending a bit of time puttering about in a tinnie, you should consider a safety floatation device for your dog like the Marlin Australia PFD dog floatation vest from BCF; bcf.com.au.

Muk Mat

Not just for pets, this mobile patch of fake grass helps to stop dirt and grit getting into the car or caravan. You can keep one in the boot to roll out and help clean off sandy paws, or buy a Muk Mat shaped like the steps of your van; mukmat.com.

Collapsible dog water bowls

Yes, a bucket will suffice, but if you are camping and want to save on space these dog bowls are a great idea. The Prima Pets collapsible silicone bowl is a compact design that folds down to just over a centimetre thick and holds a cup and a half of water, which is okay for small to medium dogs; prima-pets.com. For larger dogs the Zenify bowl holds a litre of water; zenifypets.com.au.

Dexas MudBuster

Also taking the place of a bucket, these new gadgets look a bit like a plastic drinking glass with soft teeth inside, or the mouth of some kind of sci-fi worm. You put your dog's paw in and rotate gently and the silicone bristles clean your dog's paws to get rid of all the sand, mud and dirt and it pulls apart to clean easily; themudbuster.com.

Dog hammock

To keep your back seats clean you can try a complete covering like the Pawmanity deluxe dog hammock that turns your back seat into a mobile dog hammock, presuming you don't have to fit any other passengers in on the back seat; pawmanity.com.au.

Security camera

If you do need to leave your dog for short stints, whether it is secured safely in a pen in the shade or inside a caravan with the temperature control sorted, you can invest in a security cam so you can keep an eye on things. The Orion Smart HD Grid camera from Bunnings connects to your smartphone and even has a two-way audio so your pet can hear your voice if they need to. It is not recommended as a babysitter for long stints but can provide peace of mind if you are just gone for a short time and your pup is safe and sound; bunnings.com.au.

Crate cover

This can help calm a nervous dog in the car, but make sure you get a cover with side flaps that can open to allow a free flow of air.

Canvassing opinion: deciding whether you roll in a tent, car or van

There is no right way to travel with your pet, just a lot of different decisions and compromises you need to make along the way. Whether you decide to camp, caravan or just skip between pet-friendly accommodation in the car will be the result of how much you want to spend, the length of time on the road and personal preferences.

Some people love the feeling of just canvas between them and the stars at night, others like to have a mobile ensuite, and still others prefer to have the full facilities of a pet-friendly hotel.

When it comes to camping there is a certain freedom to just having a tent and a vehicle. You will be able to go places that vans cannot and have a bit more spontaneity in where you stop and there is no doubt that camping is one of the most dog-friendly accommodation options.

For vans, you have a bit of added security with a lockable house attached to the back of your car. There is also less hassle in setting up each time you arrive at a campsite and you can even have your own, albeit basic, bathroom facilities.

If you are thinking of a mobile home, you have more comfort again; in fact, road tripping in a motorhome is a great option for long haul but it too has its drawbacks. With your home and car fused together, a quick trip to the shops means that you have to take the whole house with you, unless you have such a pro set-up that you have a bike or motorbike (or sometimes even a small car) attached to the back.

For short trips or splashing the cash, dog-friendly accommodation means you do not have to take anything but a car and a bag, but the huge downside is the scarcity of houses and hotels that will allow pets, meaning you will need to do a lot of planning and count out a huge swathe of this wide brown land.

Let's dive into a few options for life on the road.

The mobile dog home: the ABC of RVs

If you do plan to buy an RV for your doggy road trip you should be aware that they come in several basic forms, each with their advantages and disadvantages. But they all have one thing in common: their greatest strength – the mobility to live life on the road with you and your pooch – is also their greatest weakness.

Depending on how often you're on the road, and for how long, your RV is going to be exposed to stresses and forces that are the equivalent of exposing a house to regular earth tremors as you bounce along the freeway.

Of course, they are built for this, but these stresses and the inevitable damage and wear and tear will determine how long your RV lasts and in what condition you arrive home. How often you travel is a big factor because every time you set up and set down that's more wear and tear.

The big lesson here is that like everything else, the better you treat it the longer it's going to last. The way you interact with your RV on a day-to-day basis will be a major factor in the longevity of your RV. Treat your vehicle with respect, give it what it needs and prepare it properly for what you will be demanding of it. Do all that and there's every reason to believe that your RV will last longer.

The types of RV: Motorhomes (Class A)

Motorhomes are the largest RVs. They are fully integrated, one-piece units where you simply pull up at the campground and plug in the electricity: job done. The largest motorhomes, known as 'Class As', are limited to being 2.5 metres (8.2 feet) before they become classified as 'wide loads' and require special permits to be on the road. There are also smaller Class Cs and Class Bs although, funnily enough, the Class Cs are larger than the Class Bs. Class Bs are often referred to as 'campervans'.

Motorhomes can run on petrol or diesel, and some are now available that run on LPG or have LPG as a backup. The main advantage of diesel is that they require less maintenance, fewer things can go wrong with a diesel engine, and they have more torque for grinding their way up hills.

Despite their size, you don't need a special licence to drive most motorhomes.

Campervans (Class B)

The campervan is the smallest of the integrated, self-contained, one-piece motorhomes. As the name implies, campervans are built on a van chassis and their size makes them easy to handle, drive and set up at a campsite. They are still expensive, compared to cars, but much cheaper to run, maintain and repair than Class As and Class Cs. They're small enough that daytrips and excursions are a no-brainer.

A well-designed campervan will give you access to the basic amenities that make life comfortable and they will be easier to drive than a larger motorhome. They are a great starter van for dipping your toe into van life.

On the downside, campervans have limited interior space, which isn't necessarily a bad thing if you're travelling in good weather but can be really hellish if things turn inclement and you are shacked up with a very frustrated dog trying to chew its way through the van door (this has actually happened). The same goes for limited storage. What you gain in convenience you lose in amenities like cooking, cleaning and storage capacity.

Motorhomes (Class C)

These are built on a truck chassis and typically have an extension built over the main driving cabin that usually has a 'loft' sleeping area or storage area. They tend to look boxy, rather than aerodynamic but they're built for comfort and practicality, not for speed.

These vehicles have many of the advantages of Class As but with

much lower purchase, maintenance and running costs.

This class can still be expensive to maintain and operate and requires better-than-basic driving skills but they have enough space for you, and there's room for your dog to have their own private corner too.

Towable RVs

The great advantage of the towable RVs is that they separate the motoring functions from the living functions. The result is a home that can't go anywhere under its own power, and reversing can be a pain in the neck, but you can just jump in the car and go to the shops without losing your camp spot. The towable RV's flexibility is what makes them attractive, but there are a few things to consider that are universal to all towables.

You will need a car that is powerful enough to pull the full load, not just an empty RV, but an RV full of all the stuff that you're taking, including the maximum number of people and animals that you could conceivably have on board. This car will not be cheap, so factor that cost in.

Towing is a driving skillset all on its own and requires learning new techniques and lots of practice, but there are courses that can help the novice nomad.

Caravans, travel trailers and camper trailers

These are probably the first thing that comes to mind when you think 'towable RVs'. The range of size and quality is huge, from compact basic to elaborate, multi-axelled state-of-the-art 'rigs'. The range of shapes is surprising, from the smaller, aerodynamic teardrops – think the classic silver Airstream vintage caravans – to square and chunky houses on wheels. They are much less expensive than motorhomes of equivalent sizes – sometimes as little as half the cost – but you have to factor in the cost of your towing vehicle, which can really blow the cost out.

Tent trailers, fold downs and expandables

As the name implies these are trailer/tent hybrids. The trailer itself is a fixed size in a rigid frame, but the usable living space is increased when you deploy tent-like extensions. They're basically a large tent in their own easily transportable box so they tend to suit the more outdoorsy types that are used to tents anyway.

Some of the positive features include their small size and light weight that make them easy to manoeuvre. They can be towed even by a normal, family sedan car and they're also relatively inexpensive to buy, maintain and repair.

But you pay for all those pluses with a very limited interior and storage so you have to pack smart. They're also more exposed to the weather, so they might not be suitable for extreme conditions. Be prepared to have a dog in your sleeping bag if the thunder and lightning starts.

Down to the bone: how to keep a tight budget on a pet road trip

Road tripping with your dog will be an amazing experience but you need to make sure it is not one that costs you a fortune – unless of course you have that sort of money to throw around, in which case 'well done you!'

Your three biggest costs will be fuel, food and accommodation, most likely in that order, so make sure you make smart choices on all these fronts and you will be able to travel for a lot longer.

Your overall budget should take into account the following basics:

- Fuel
- Groceries and food (for you and your pooch)
- Camping/van fees or accommodation costs
- Insurance and vehicle registration
- Equipment: both before you go and stuff you find you need when travelling
- Entertainment: attractions, tours, activities and entry fees
- Laundry, if you are not in a van
- Car ferries
- Vehicle parts and services
- Pet sitting: for when your pooch needs to be parked
- Vet fees: both regular checks if you are away that long or a budget for pet emergencies that might crop up as you travel

Be prepared

Vehicle costs and breakdowns can be the biggest part of a road trip budget, so get your vehicle fully serviced before you go. Having a newly serviced car or van will save you worry, but more importantly it can save on costs in the long run.

A well-serviced vehicle uses less fuel so make sure you have your tyres at the correct inflation and a full oil change to have your car running smoothly. Budget for regular services on the road if you are away for a long time. Being proactive saves money and it might also save you being stuck on the side of the road with steam pouring out of your poor engine as your pup looks on dumbfounded.

Deciding where and when to go

You might be able to afford to see the whole of Australia, but if you can't you will have to prioritise the things you want to see. Make a list of the must-see spots and see how many you can afford to visit. If you have the freedom, make sure you avoid peak times like warmer weather, public holidays and school holidays when prices are inflated on where you stay and what you eat. Travelling off-peak can be a great way to see more.

Plan your meals

Most people can't afford to eat out every day on a huge road trip, so you will need to plan what you eat, and stock up at the shops when you can, particularly if you are going far from convenience stores. If you do eat out, make sure it is worth it. Don't waste money on average meals when you are on a budget; do some planning and make your meals out memorable, or save eating out for when you really can't be bothered to make something for yourself.

You will need to have a budget for all your expenses and for food you will need a daily budget based on the planned number of times you are going to eat out and the cost of your daily meals in the van or at the campground. This may be a good time to embrace home brands, to know what is in season and therefore cheaper, and make things you would normally buy like pasta sauce and salad dressing.

And be sure to pack snacks to avoid buying expensive and unhealthy servo food every time you get a grumbling tummy.

Skip the cities – and the boonies

Everything costs more in the big smoke, so unless you really must head into the capital cities steer clear of the higher costs of living. If you need a city fix, make sure you park or camp on the outskirts and maybe get some dog minding while you commute in to do what you need to.

Costs also tend to soar in really remote places as well, given the cost of transporting food and fuel to these parts. You want to stick to the 'Goldilocks zone' between the cities and the far reaches of the outback – not too urban, not too remote, just right.

Play by the rules

Don't speed or break any road rules because a fine can put a serious dent in even the best-planned budgets.

Take a water bottle

This will be basic to anyone who already camps but if you buy water it adds up to some serious costs in the long run and is not very sustainable either.

Plan your route carefully

Listen to your GPS, plan ahead and don't take the long way around (unless there is something amazing you want to see that way) and you will save on petrol and vehicle wear and tear. This might not be a race, but planning your trip will save time and money, and it need not reduce the discovery and fun; after all, that is why you left home in the first place. Try to avoid toll roads where possible, you are not in a hurry.

Don't fill up on the freeway

Those hulking servos are convenient all right, and they charge you for it. If you are on the road long term you need to plan your petrol stops and make sure they are good value for money. You can use an app like GasBuddy, a US app that now works in Australia, to find the best prices near you.

And this might be a good time to pay attention to the fuel vouchers

that come on the back of some supermarket receipts (although, pay attention to the price and be aware that any savings may be outweighed by a higher price per litre).

Splurge selectively

Attractions are just like meals: if you are going to splash out and see something make sure it is worth it. And if it is not dog-friendly then you will need to factor in the price of finding some local dog sitting.

Don't skimp either. If you drove to Broken Hill just to see the *Mad Max 2* museum now is not the time to save money and give it a miss. There is a Goldilocks zone for finances, too.

As part of your trip planning, make sure you include as many free attractions and activities as you can. There are whole books and websites dedicated to fee-free attractions so make sure you know where they are at your next stop and whether a dog can come with you, of course.

Keep your valuables secure

Ideally, leave your valuables at home (you're not going to need fancy jewellery while on the road!) but it's likely that on most trips you will have high-value equipment like laptops, mobile phones, and camera gear with you, as well as other essentials like bikes, a portable fridge, a barbecue or even an esky full of food that can be expensive and inconvenient to replace.

If you are camping it will be harder to protect your valuables but if you are not going to be around the campsite lock anything you don't want to lose in your car. You should also consider using locks or lockable cables with valuable items you can't fit in your car and don't want to lose.

When travelling with an RV or van close the curtains when you're away from it to help conceal your computers and technology from prying eyes. Make sure you stash expensive items out of sight if you do need to leave them in your vehicle.

If you are able to customise your vehicle you can have hidden or lockable compartments added for storing valuable items. Otherwise, lockable storage boxes can be a good deterrent.

Create a separate pet budget

Take a note of monthly expenses, including treats, toys and grooming. You will need to stick to a budget on the road so consider making your own treats (there are plenty of recipes online) and if you have a dog that likes to wrestle or play with things you can knot your own ropes or even use old clothing. Your dog is getting the experiences of their lifetime on the great open road so go easy on the rest of the spoiling.

Keep an eye on dental health (yours and your dog's!)

This can be a big cost, and one not covered by a lot of insurance policies, so make sure you get your pet used to regular brushing on the road and you will reduce the risk of a big vet bill.

CHAPTER TWO

DOG SAFETY

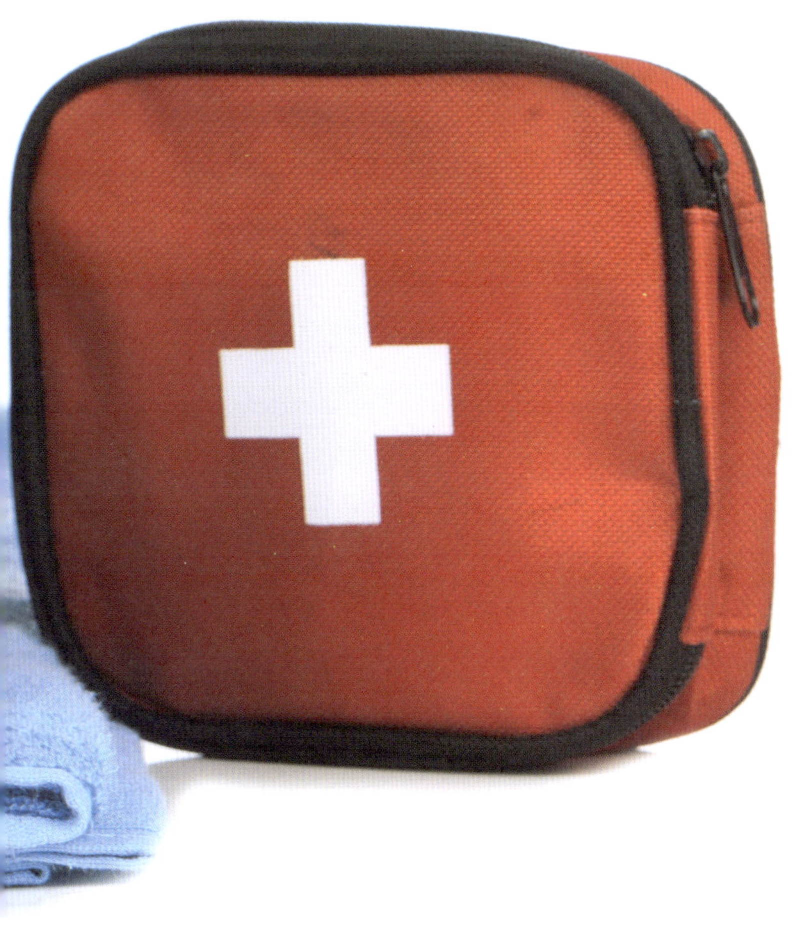

Doctor Spot: caring for your carefree canine

When it comes to healthy road tripping with your dog, veterinarian Tania Mullen from Essendon Vet Clinic in Melbourne's west warns travellers that dogs, just like humans, can vary in how car sick they get.

'If you find that your dog does get car sick there are medications that your vet can prescribe to help with this,' Mullen says. 'Then we suggest a trial run before travelling so you can ensure the medication works and that you get the dose right.'

Even if your dog does not get sick, she recommends gradually desensitising your dog to car rides, starting with small trips and working up to longer ones. You might even begin by just sitting in a stationary car with your dog and giving it some treats and positive reinforcement. If your pet does get carsick your vet can prescribe Cerenia, which lasts for 24 hours. The more natural, over-the-counter options are not quite as effective.

Mullen says you can use sedatives for a particularly anxious pet, but only on car rides. Sedatives are not recommended for plane trips due to the high mortality rate.

Mullen suggests travellers get the basics right first. Things like a safety belt and harness, making sure you take enough breaks for water and exercise, and ensuring your heartworm and vaccinations are up to date. She also suggests communicating with the local vets in an area that you are staying in.

'Call into the local vet to find out what problems are common in the area,' she says. 'Is this an area that has ticks, or has a higher risk of heartworm? Also, you should know where the 24-hour vet clinics are in your area, and some clinics will have an on-call service in rural Australia.

'If your pet has a chronic disease it is a good idea to get a vet check-up prior to going. You can get your history either emailed to you or to a particular vet clinic so that all relevant information is accessible as you travel.'

And if your animal has a chronic ailment that requires regular medication make sure you have enough prescriptions to take with you, or arrange with your vet to have a bulk supply of six months worth of meds that you can pack up in a medical kit.

First aid on the road

Head veterinarian at Vetwest Animal Hospitals in Perth, Yolande Oosthuizen, says that travellers should be aware of a new disease affecting dogs in the north of Australia, spread by the brown dog tick. Canine ehrlichiosis is spread through the bite of a bacterium-carrying tick and can cause lethargy, loss of appetite, joint swelling and difficulty breathing. If not caught early the disease can be fatal.

'How you prevent it is to make sure that your animal has flea and tick prevention on board,' Oosthuizen says. 'You can get a Seresto collar which is quite good because the tick does not have to bite to be killed off.'

Ticks start quite small and then grow as they suck blood. Once they are swollen and engorged they can be easier to see. What you need to do if you find a tick is to remove the whole thing completely. Paralysis ticks exist in certain parts of the country and the way to remove them is to get small forceps or prongs with a 90-degree edge that you push under the mouthparts of the tick then twist to remove the little parasite. Signs of a tick might include a fever, lack of energy and vitality, or just being unwell or off their food.

Oosthuizen says that when it comes to first aid, similar principles apply for dogs and humans. It is about treating any wounds correctly, applying pressure if there is any bleeding and being careful not to get injured yourself while you are trying to help an injured pet.

'Even the sweetest little dog, if they are sore, can bite,' she says. 'People will tell you "my dog would never bite" but if they have a wound and are hurt any dog can bite.'

Put saline or clean water on a wound to get rid of any dirt or dust. And if you are travelling near a beach be sure to keep the dog off the sand because a wound full of sand won't heal properly.

'Make sure the dog doesn't lick the area,' she adds, 'It is an old wives' tale that letting a dog lick its wound will help to make it better. Their mouths are not the cleanest and it doesn't work like that. For this reason I suggest that people travel with a first-aid kit and they have a bucket collar in it to stop the licking.'

In the case of a snake bite, Oosthuizen says the current advice is to not get the animal worked up or excited, they need to be kept calm.

'Before, they said to apply tourniquets to the bite, but that is not as important as not getting them worked up so it is better to just keep them calm and not get the blood flowing too quickly, then get straight to a vet.'

When it comes to baits or poison, the best advice is preventative. Be aware of areas that might be trying to bait wild dogs and consider a muzzle if your dog is prone to scavenging for food.

'The main bait they put out is called 1080,' says Oosthuizen. 'And if they have eaten it there is very little that can be done. If you are in an area with 1080 make sure your dog is on a lead and keep it out of bushland. If you know they have eaten it you must get to a vet straight away. If we get to them soon enough we can make them vomit but sometimes even with that they have absorbed enough for it to be fatal. Baits are very good at doing the job they were designed for.'

Local government will often post in the local press where they are actively baiting but it is a good idea to simply be on guard the whole time you are travelling in remote areas.

Yolande Oosthuizen's top travel tips

Oosthuizen travelled with her staffy Varkie (Afrikaans for 'piglet') all over WA for years in a camper trailer.

Find the space in the car where your dog is the most comfortable. Some dogs like the footwell, others like to see what is going on outside, find the place where your dog is happy.

Stop often for them to spread their legs. Every two hours is a good amount of time.

Plan before you go, because a lot of national parks do not allow dogs. 'We have made that mistake before, travelling to the Pinnacles and then not being allowed in,' she says.

Patching up Patch: the ultimate travel first-aid kit

If you are going to be travelling for any length of time then you should have a first-aid kit on board, for humans and animals.

If you are somewhere remote, your first-aid kit and your first-aid skills can literally save the life of your pet. A trip to the vet may be too late for a dog that is bleeding out, choking, or has stopped breathing. The better your kit, and the more up-to-date your first-aid training, the better chance your dog has at surviving. Both the Red Cross and the RSPCA offer short courses on pet first aid where you can learn a range of handy skills to help save a life. Some of the courses are even available via webinar so find a campground with some solid wifi and you can be a first-aid expert in no time.

Your pet first-aid kit will need to have items that can help you stop bleeding, stabilise a fractured limb, respond to poisons where possible and manage eye wounds. You can buy first-aid kits from places like FurSafe (fursafe.com.au) that are pre-made with the basics or you can tailor your kit to your dog's specific needs.

The contents of any kit will depend on how long you are away, where you are going and what the needs of your dog are, but we have some suggestions:

Bandages

For any unexpected cuts or scratches you will need bandages like the GMV Medi-Vet bandages that are elastic and easily tear off. And make sure you have medical-grade tape to secure the bandages. They can be handy for a range of reasons including bite injuries, serious cuts, or even caltrop (three-corner jack), a noxious spiny burr that can injure paws and is prevalent in the Kimberley, Katherine and north Queensland.

Antiseptic

Treat the wound with an antiseptic whether it is simple hydrogen peroxide, betadine, a saline wash or something like Rufus & Coco's Antiseptic Aid that has Vitamin E and aloe vera to help soothe abrasions and bites; rufusandcoco.com.au.

Antibiotic allergy cream

If your dog is sensitive to grass and prone to skin conditions then this is a must to have with you.

Eye/snout cream

If you are travelling north, the heat and dust can affect your dog's eyes and also chap and crack your dog's nose. Pack something like Natural Dog Company's Snout Soother Stick from Raw and Fresh; rawandfresh.com.au.

Ear drops

Treat ear infections on the go with something like the Epi-Otic ear and skin cleanser for dogs; petbarn.com.au.

Tweezers/scissors

For removing ticks and splinters from your dog's skin and paws you will require tweezers, and scissors can help trim fur or remove damaged skin.

Antihistamines

You can use over-the-counter allergy drugs for your dog like Polaramine, Phenergan or Telfast, but check with your vet for the recommended dosages for your pet.

Thermometer

A flexible digital thermometer can help to tell if your dog has a fever or if it is suffering from heat stroke.

Splint

KRUUSE offer a variety of splints from Quicksplints for emergency treatment of wounds and breaks to aluminium options that can be bent and cut to the right size; provet.com.au.

Emergency thermal blanket

Packing something like a Mylar thermal blanket can help your dog conserve body heat to prevent hypothermia in the cold or stop your dog from going into shock in emergency situations; petevacpak.com.

Rubber gloves

Even pets need to be protected from infection, so use gloves if you have an open wound that needs treating so you keep any wounds clear of bacteria.

Soda crystals/emetic

In the event your dog has been poisoned you might not have time for the vet to induce vomiting so carry some Lectric washing soda crystals (sodium carbonate). Use 3–5 crystals then walk the dog around until they vomit; make sure you discuss how to use this safely with your vet before you leave home.

Super glue

This may sound odd, but it can act in much the same way as surgeon's use glue to close a wound. For emergency use only but it is still good to have on hand.

Styptic pencil

This is a medicated stick made from powdered crystals that can help seal small wounds.

Stingose/white vinegar

Treatment for bites or stings while out playing.

Collar dangers

You will want your dog to have a collar when they are away with you but there are a number of dangers posed by collars. When dogs are playing their jaws have been known to get stuck behind a collar and that can injure or even dislocate the jaw. A dog can get snagged on unfamiliar bushes and be choked to death. Or your dog could simply get snagged far from home and be unable to return to you.

The KeepSafe Break-Away Collar is one option to make sure this does not happen to your dog. The collar was made after research discovering that at least half of all dog owners had experienced at least one collar-related incident, so the manufacturers designed a collar that will simply break away when it comes under too much pressure.

When walking your dog, the lead is looped through two metal D-rings so it cannot break off, but when the D-rings are unhooked from the lead there is a breakaway buckle that releases when pressure is applied; au.petsafe.net.

TRAVEL TAILS

Sam and George Miller, and Frankie the whippet

Frankie's first big road trip went from Sydney down the south coast of New South Wales and through to the Victorian goldfields.

'It is really hard to leave your dog behind,' says Sam Miller. 'The thing with dogs is they love you so much and that undiluted adoration is something that is very hard to part with.'

Miller accepts that there are some restrictions when travelling with dogs but she enjoys the fact that you holiday differently. The need to find dog-friendly situations means that you have to research ahead of time and that ends up uncovering things you might not normally find. For Miller that means that one of the first stops anywhere is the information centre, which will often have a clear list of where dogs are allowed. The Millers have been surprised by how dog-accepting some places can be.

'The best place for dogs that we went on this trip was Ballarat,' Miller says. 'Ballarat is not very crowded and we stayed at this caravan park with a new innovation.'

Big4 Ballarat Windmill Holiday Park has new fenced areas where you can back your caravan into the area, slide a door shut and then you have parked your mobile home inside your very own dog park. This way you can simply open the door and let your dog out to go to the toilet, or relax next to the van with a coffee. There are also plans to build a dog run.

Miller loved walking Frankie around Lake Wendouree with a stop at Pipers by the Lake that has a great dog-friendly area. 'We met a group of greyhound rescue people who had about 15 greyhounds there and Frankie was very keen on all the greyhounds,' she says. 'She thinks she might be a greyhound when she grows up but she is mistaken.' Miller also recommends a walk in the Botanical Gardens.

There was one incident on the road trip where Frankie got a urinary tract infection, and Miller learned an interesting lesson. 'It was Saturday morning and it was very hard to get into a local vet, so we rang our vet who was able to email a prescription for antibiotics through to us that my husband picked up. So you can do things like that if you are in a bind.'

Pooch pinching: stopping your dog from getting stolen

Dog theft is on the rise with more dogs getting stolen more often. Many breeds are still hot property after the crazy dog bull-market that was 2020, when the costs of dogs – and therefore their likelihood of getting nicked – skyrocketed, as every man and their, well, dog, wanted to secure a pet.

A lot of places don't allow pets near camp kitchens or toilet blocks, and if you are travelling alone with your dog you may have no-one to mind them when you go to the shops, or even just leave them for a few minutes.

If you are travelling in a campervan in the warmer months and you need to leave your dog in a van while you take a quick trip to the shower or toilet, make sure you have a second key to your vehicle. You can leave the engine idling, and keep the air conditioning running, so your dog is safe and does not overheat. Ditto the cold, though very few places in Australia get so cold as to pose any danger.

If your dog can be seen you may wish to leave a note with your phone number saying where you are and when you left, as a well-meaning passer-by might break into the car thinking the dog is in danger. And remember, you should only leave your dog unattended for short periods of time; this is not a doggy daycare substitute. In almost all states it is illegal to leave your dog alone for even a short amount of time in a car, even with the aircon running, so make sure you know the rules.

If your dog is crate trained, one tip is to leave them in the crate while you are away and travel with padlocks, one to lock the door of the crate and another to secure it to the van or something that thieves cannot easily transport.

For those travelling by car that just need to leave their dog unattended briefly at the shops or other venue there are also lockable leads. SafelySecured is a lockable lead and harness that has stainless steel cables stitched inside the material and a combination lock to attach your dog to something sturdy. It's an Australian invention that has come about precisely because of the current market value of your travelling companion; safely-secured.com.

Sitting pretty: getting your dog minded on the road

No matter how much time you want to spend with your best furry friend, there will be times that you need to go places where your dog is not allowed. Whether it is a day trip to a national park, an art gallery, or just a trip to the shops there are a few options when it comes to finding dog-sitting on an extended holiday.

Trawling Facebook for groups like Travelling with Dogs Australia, Pet Sitting Australia, and the various state-based offshoots with a similar theme is a good place to start with many people offering to look after pets for people who are stuck. There is also Van Life Pet Tenders and a series of local community pages for the areas you will be travelling in.

If you are spending a while at the same caravan park you could put up flyers or simply network your way into some pet sitting, or offer it on a quid-pro-quo basis to other dog owners that you meet and trust.

Nationally, if you want to keep things professional you can sign up to Mad Paws, PetCloud or Pawshake. These are all services that offer a database of sitters in your area that will either come for a day or even stay over and mind your pet overnight. These carers are all rated and have had their credentials checked by the sites. These sites are generally more concentrated on offering services in the cities but it is still worth checking out as you never know when someone might be signed up nearby who can give you a bit more freedom as you drive around.

Dog minding should be around $20 for the day in the regions but can rise to $50 at doggy daycare centres in the major cities. Given that big cities are where you are most likely to need a bit more freedom you might also consider using these services on a half-day or full-day casual rate.

Most are easy to sign up to as long as you have proof of vaccination.

Just make sure anyone that you leave your dog with is a registered business. They need to have an ABN and in some states they also need a domestic animals business licence.

DOGS
MUST BE
ON A
LEAD

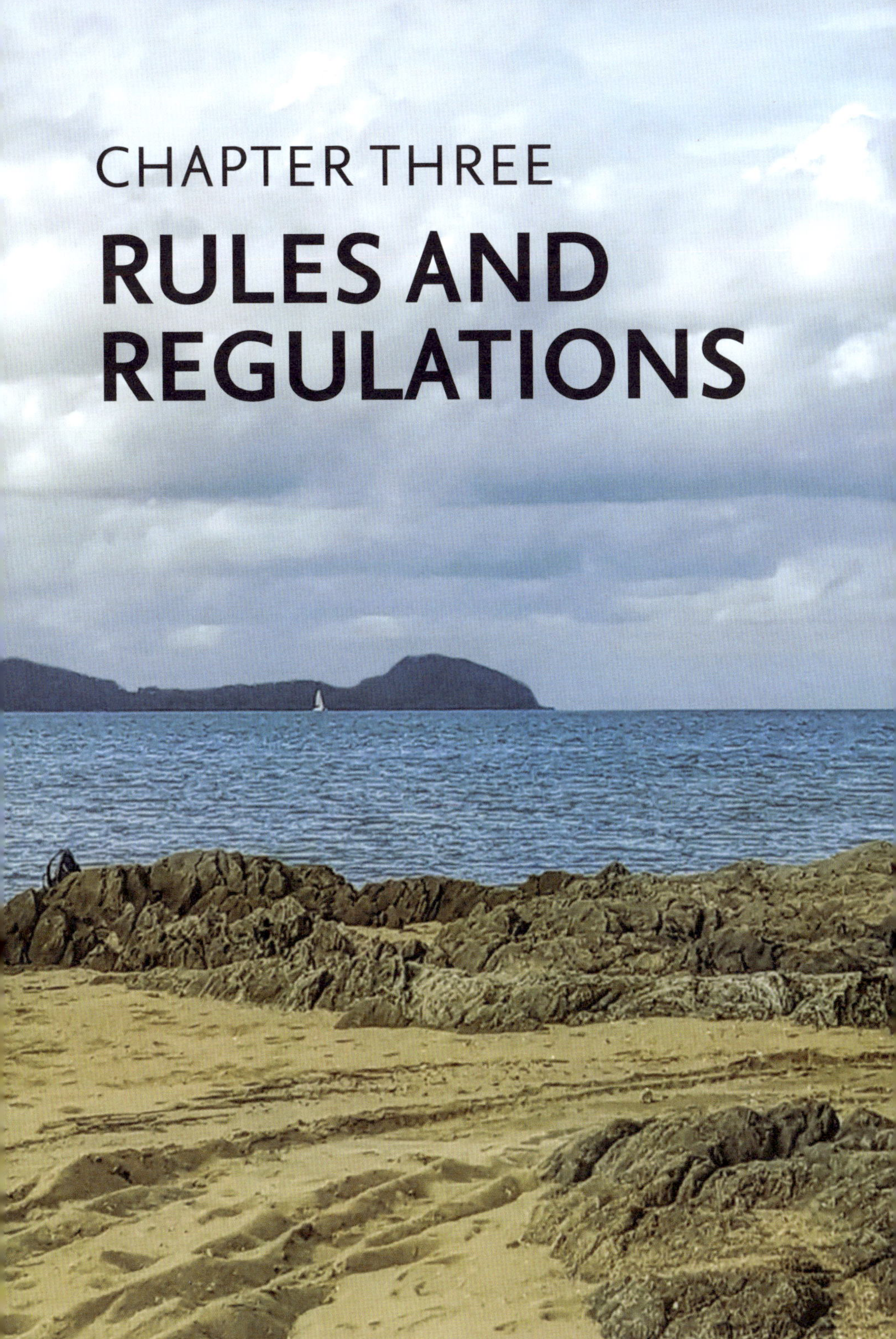

CHAPTER THREE

RULES AND REGULATIONS

Legal beagle: dogs and the law when you travel

Most of the legal ramifications for travelling with your dog are common sense. They relate to the various animal cruelty acts passed at a state level and cover things like providing enough food, water and protection when you are on holidays – but they also cover how your dog travels in your car, ute or van with you.

For example, it is illegal in most states for your pet to travel in the boot of your car and in Victoria you cannot leave a dog unattended for more than 10 minutes in a car where the outside heat is higher than 28 degrees.

Some states, like WA, have a rule where the dog cannot be in a position where they 'could distract or obstruct the vision of the driver', this is a broader power so if the dog was to be found unrestrained on the back seat it could be argued they were a distraction. A dog is not allowed on the driver's lap in the west either, which seems like a pretty good idea.

Queensland and the Northern Territory also favour a broader legal definition when it comes to travelling with your dog. They make it illegal for a pet to be transported in any way that is detrimental to its health and welfare, or that may cause the animal suffering.

There is a very good reason why the majority of states make it a legal requirement for a dog to be restrained when the car is moving, either by a device that clips into the seatbelt buckle or connects to the existing seatbelts in the car. Movies and TV shows may show blue heelers sitting next to their owner on the passenger seat of beat-up trucks as they drive on desert tracks at sunset but the reality is that if you do not have a movie dog that is perfectly trained that dog could be a distraction.

If you have an accident an unrestrained dog could become a very dangerous projectile that could harm you and the dog. A dog that is not restrained could also jump out of an open window and harm itself or another road user.

You must also restrain dogs when they travel in the back of a ute or open-backed truck. If your pet is travelling in a pet transport crate it is the crate that must be secured to stop it sliding around or causing distraction. Most states will fine you and deduct demerit points if they believe that the way you are transporting your pet is in any way detrimental to your driving. And if your pet is injured as a result of your negligence you may face fines and prosecution under the state's animal protection act.

To be completely up to speed with the latest laws check the roads and traffic authority in the various states that you are spending time in.

Since your pup is family, the best idea is simply to buckle them up the same way you would the rest of the pack.

Dogs might fly: when the road runs out

Usually flying is just for pet transport, but if you are not driving all the way you might need to all hop a plane to get to your final destination.

However, Australia is a long way off other parts of the world when it comes to flying with dogs and cats. You will not see pets in the cabin like you will in the US or parts of Europe, although properly trained and licensed service dogs are allowed.

In the past you could not even guarantee that your pet would be on the same flight as you, they would simply be sent in the cargo without you, like a package, and you would be advised on when and where to pick them up. Now you can fly with your pet but it is suggested you book the pet transport first and then book your own seat on a plane, not the other way around, as there are less places in the hold than up above, so your pet's seat will be harder to find.

Check with each individual airline about their rules if you are planning to take to the skies.

Salty old sea dogs: taking your pup on the boat to Tasmania

If you are heading off the Australian mainland the beauty about going to Tassie on the *Spirit of Tasmania* ferry is that your fur baby can come along with you. They are not exactly by your side but located in kennels on the ventilated decks (decks 3 and 5) of the *Spirit of Tasmania*.

You cannot visit your dog as you sail but the crew checks on them regularly and makes sure they have a steady supply of fresh water. If your pet has a medical condition that requires more attention, you must get a letter from your vet and you will be allowed to have escorted visits to the kennels to attend to your dog's medical needs. Kennels vary in size but the approximate measurements are 700 mm wide x 800 mm high x 900 mm deep.

The kennels are a basic set-up without beds, so it is recommended you bring bedding if your pet requires it, plus something familiar might help with the separation from you.

It is also recommended that your pet is well exercised prior to boarding, and not given any solid food just prior to sailing just in case

they are prone to getting seasick; the seas on the way over to the Apple Isle can challenge the hardiest of sailors on a bad night so be prepared, for you and your dog.

It is advisable to consult your veterinarian prior to travel. They will be able to confirm your pet is fit to travel and provide further advice about preparing your pet for sea travel. They might even offer some prescription drugs to assist you with the journey.

All dogs entering Tasmania are subject to biosecurity entry conditions and must be treated for hydatid tapeworm within 14 days prior to entering Tasmania. Documentary evidence of this treatment must be carried by whoever accompanies the dog into Tasmania and presented for inspection when you get there.

The evidence can be:

- An official statement/certificate by a vet;
- A statutory declaration by the owner; or
- Other evidence of treatment (such as the pill packet and purchase receipt, though the first two are definitely stronger evidence and the preferable way to go).

Park life: dogs and national parks

Some of the most beautiful places in Australia are cared for by the national parks authorities in each state and territory, and they do an amazing job of maintaining our natural wonders and wildlife. However, dogs are not allowed into most national parks, nature reserves and state recreation parks in Australia.

Dogs have the potential to scare or even kill local wildlife if they are not properly controlled, and even the scent of a dog can cause chaos for our local birds and animals. Dogs can also damage the plants in a national park and if you dog is lost it can become part of the feral dog problem that many parks have.

So, if you are dead keen on seeing something contained in a national park, and that includes some beautiful beaches, you will have to leave your dog behind. You can drive through a national park on a public road with your pet in tow but the dog must remain inside the vehicle. There are a limited number of camp sites inside national parks that allow dogs but they must be on a lead at all times. There are a few exceptions that we have rounded up below on a state-by-state basis. To make sure you are on top of any changes you can head to the various state parks websites for the most up-to-date information.

Australian Capital Territory

In the ACT, dogs are prohibited in all national parks as well as several significant nature reserves (Black Mountain, Callum Brae (Mt Mugga Mugga), Crace Grasslands, Dunlop Grasslands, Goorooyaroo, Gungaderra, Jerrabomberra Wetlands, McQuoids Hill, Mullangarri Grasslands, Mulligans Flat and Rob Roy). There are a few on-lead exceptions such as O'Connor/Bruce Ridge, Mt Ainslie, Mt Majura, Tuggeranong Hill, Wanniassa Hills, Farrer Ridge, Mt Taylor and Red Hill.

New South Wales

Some historic sites, such as Hill End Historic Site and Hartley Historic Site, are managed as 'living' villages or towns. Pet dogs may be permitted on-lead in these locations, including associated campgrounds.

Berowra Valley Regional Park, Sydney

On-lead dogs are permitted on the Bellamy trail between Bellamy Street and De Saxe Close, Thornleigh; Daphne trail between Tuscan Way (at the end of Daphne Close) and Patricia Place, Cherrybrook; and Clarinda trail, between Clarinda Street and Simon Place, Hornsby.

Blue Gum Hills Regional Park, Newcastle

On-lead dogs are permitted away from picnic areas and children's play areas.

Bomaderry Creek Regional Park

On-lead dogs permitted away from picnic areas and children's play areas.

Coffs Coast Regional Park

On-lead dogs permitted at Hearns Lake Beach (Woolgoolga), Darkum Beach (Woolgoolga North), Corindi/Pipe Clay Beach (Arrawarra North), Emerald Beach, north of Fiddamans Creek and south of Diggers Head, Woolgoolga Back Beach, Woolgoolga Lake.

Euston Regional Park

On-lead dogs permitted in all areas.

Goolawah Regional Park

On-lead dogs permitted at Delicate campground and Delicate Beach.

Leacock Regional Park, Sydney

On-lead dogs permitted in all areas.

Murray Valley Regional Park

Dogs permitted in all areas.

Murrumbidgee Valley Regional Park

Dogs permitted at Bunyip Hole campground and Wooloondool campground.

Parramatta River Regional Park, Sydney

On-lead dogs permitted on designated walking tracks in the park and in the nearby foreshore parks to the east and west.

Rouse Hill Regional Park, Sydney

On-lead dogs permitted in all areas except hired pavilions and children's play areas.

William Howe Regional Park, Sydney

On-lead dogs permitted in all areas.

Wolli Creek Regional Park, Sydney

Dogs permitted in all areas.

Worimi Regional Park, Newcastle

On-lead dogs permitted on a 3-kilometre section of the beach south of Birubi Headland.

Yellomundee Regional Park, Blue Mountains

On-lead dogs permitted on Coreena and Burrawang bridle trails and Transgrid management trail along the Nepean River.

Northern Territory

On-the-spot fines apply in the NT, and with vast swathes of natural wonders there are only a few options for dog owners.

Alice Springs region

You can visit with your dog at Owen Springs Reserve. Dogs are allowed south of the Waterhouse Range and may camp with you at Redbank Waterhole campground.

Casuarina Coastal Reserve, Darwin
Both on- and off-lead options with signs clearly marking them.

Charles Darwin National Park, Darwin
Dogs are allowed on the sealed roads and car parks but are not allowed in the picnic area or on mountain bike trails.

George Brown Darwin Botanic Gardens
Signs clearly show on-lead areas.

Holmes Jungle Nature Park, Darwin
You can take your dog on the walking tracks and have them in car parks.

Queensland

Most parks in the sunshine state are clearly marked and there are few exceptions apart from service dogs.

Byfield State Forest
You can enjoy a picnic with your dog in the Red Rock visitor area of this popular state forest but can't go wandering too far.

Daisy Hill Conservation Park, Brisbane
Here dog owners can choose from a wide variety of tracks from an easy stroll to a decent hike with their pet.

Inskip Peninsula Recreation Area (gateway to Fraser Island)
This is a great one for dogs that love the beach.

Dog-friendly camping areas
Dogs can stay overnight in the following camping areas: Amamoor Creek camping area, Benarkin State Forest, Brooyar State Forest, Inskip Peninsula Recreation Area, Kalpowar State Forest, Wongi State Forest.

South Australia

Blackwood Forest Recreation Park may be one of the few national parks in the country where dogs are actually allowed off-lead if they are under effective control. But there are a few other walks in and around Adelaide where dogs are welcome if they are on-lead.

Anstey Hill Recreation Park

This park is not far from Adelaide and good for long walks.

Belair National Park

Bushland on-lead walking trails.

Brownhill Creek Recreation Park

On-lead offerings just 8 kilometres from Adelaide.

Cobbler Creek Recreation Park

A popular suburban park for dog walking.

Greenhill Recreation Park

A small park with views over the Adelaide Plains.

Marino Conservation Park

Costal lighthouse views and plenty of room to roam on-lead.

Morialta Conservation Park

Dogs are only allowed in the Morialta picnic area and along Morialta Falls Road to the Morialta Falls car park.

Mount George Conservation Park, Adelaide Hills

Dogs are allowed within the recreation zone between Mount George Road and Cox Creek.

O'Halloran Hill Recreation Park

Horses and dogs allowed at this park. Note, the name of the park is transitioning to Glenthorne National Park-Ityamaiitpinna Yarta.

Onkaparinga River Recreation Park

On-lease trail that includes wetland boardwalks.

Para Wirra Conservation Park

Plenty of bush at this park and a sports oval as well.

Shepherds Hill Recreation Park

Some old railway infrastructure adds some interest to this on-lead walk.

Sturt Gorge Recreation Park

A rocky walk with dogs allowed on-lead.

Totness Recreation Park, Mount Barker

Easy walking trails with on-lead access and waterside picnic areas.

Wara Wayingga-Tennyson Dunes Conservation Reserve

Get ready to dust off the sand as you come back from this reserve that has plenty of sand-dune action.

Tasmania

The stunning beauty of our southern island state is equally well protected and they are rightly concerned that any lost dog can soon turn feral and cause huge issues for Tassie's local species.

Bay of Fires Conservation Area

At this spectacular coastal park, pets are permitted on-lead and on designated walking tracks only.

Coal Mines Historic Site

Dogs are permitted on-lead.

Coles Bay Conservation Area

The area is a mix of on- and off-lead areas, as well as prohibited zones. Dogs are not permitted in nearby Freycinet National Park.

Coningham Nature Recreation Area

The area is a mix of on- and off-lead areas. The area is also used by horse-riders and it is expected that dog walkers move aside to allow horse-riders to pass and avoid disturbing the horse.

Eaglehawk Neck Historic Site

The area is a mix of on- and off-lead areas.

Evercreech (near Fingal)

Dogs are permitted on-lead.

Esperance River Picnic Area (near Dover)

Dogs are welcome and permitted off-lead, provided they stay close to their owners and are under effective control at all times.

Goblin Forest Walk (near St Helens)

Dogs are permitted on-lead.

Hogarth Falls, Strahan

Dogs are permitted on-lead and on designated walking tracks only.

Hollybank (near Launceston)

Dogs are permitted on-lead.

Kate Reed Nature Recreation Area, Launceston

Dogs are welcome but do need to be on-lead at all times to ensure the safety of other track users.

Loontitetermairrelehoiner, Swansea

Dogs are permitted on-lead, but from 15 September to 15 April, dogs are not permitted on the track between dusk and dawn due to nesting shorebirds.

Montezuma Falls

Dogs are permitted on-lead, but it is unsafe for pets to drink from or swim in the creeks due to heavy metals from historic mining.

Peter Murrell Reserves (south of Hobart)

The area is a mix of on- and off-lead areas.

Tahune Airwalk, Huon Valley

Dogs are permitted on-lead.

Trevallyn Nature Recreation Area, Launceston

On-lead dog walking is allowed is some areas of the reserve. There are maps onsite that show the different areas available to dog owners.

Dog-friendly camping areas

Dogs can stay overnight in the following camping areas: Arthur-Pieman Conservation Area, Bay of Fires Conservation Area, Humbug Point Nature Recreation Area, Peggs Beach Conservation Area, Waterhouse Conservation Area.

Victoria

Most of the general rules apply to Victorian national parks but there are a few spots where you can take your dog.

Cape Conran Coastal Park, Gippsland

This stunning coastal camping area, metres from the beach and where each camp spot has its own fire pit, allows dogs as long as they are on a lead.

Great Otway National Park

You can take your dog to a few spots on the Great Ocean Road as long as they are on a lead, such as the St George River Track near Lorne, Lake Elizabeth visitor and camping areas and walking tracks near Forrest, Ironbark Basin picnic area, Southside Beach, Addiscott Beach, Point Addis to Anglesea via beach and Surf Coast Walk, Ironbark Gorge Walking Track, Ocean View Walking Track (all near Torquay), and all of Johanna Beach. The nearby Otway Forest Park permits dogs on-lead in all areas.

Greater Bendigo National Park

Dogs are allowed on-lead on specified roads and trails in the One Tree Hill section of the park. Dog walking off these roads and trails is not permitted. Nearby Bendigo Regional Park and state forests permit dog walking. For more information, view the map of dog walking in parks and forests around Bendigo, available at parks.
vic.gov.au

Heathcote-Graytown National Park

Dogs are allowed on-lead in the McIvor Range area of the park.

Kinglake National Park

Dogs are allowed on-lead in the Frank Thomson Reserve.

Lake Eildon National Park

Dogs are allowed in the Jerusalem Creek campground.

Western Australia

The WA Parks and Wildlife Service has virtually no exceptions to its parkwide ban on all dogs except service dogs. Pets may travel in a boat in marine parks but are not allowed to enter or exit the boat within park boundaries. But there is some limited camping available.

Dog-friendly camping areas

Dogs can stay overnight in the following camping areas: Big Brook Arboretum, Blackwood River National Park, Sues Bridge, Warner Glen, Lane Poole Reserve, Baden Powell, Charlies Flat, Chuditch, Nanga Brook, Nanga Mill, Nanga Townsite, Stringers, Tonys Bend, Yarragil, Logue Brook, Rapids Conservation Park, Canebrook Pool, Stockton Lake.

TRAVEL TAILS

Sue and Maurie Fisher and Bobbie and Fancy the show Labradors

Sue Fisher has plenty of dogs to choose from to take on holidays as she and her husband raise 10 show dogs under the banner of Mikelli Labradors. But the most they have ever taken at one time is four dogs when they went up the north coast of Queensland to Darwin to visit the agricultural shows.

'That was hard work and a long time ago,' she says. 'There are a lot more places taking pets these days, in particular caravan parks.'

The Fishers travel with their dogs crated in the back of their vehicle and stay in a caravan in a mix of free camping and caravan parks. They also travel with some fencing that encircles the annex of the car so that their dogs have somewhere to 'lay down, relax and have a stretch'.

'My biggest piece of advice is to be aware of other guests,' Fisher says. 'We look for pet-friendly caravan parks but you have to make sure you check because sometimes they just allow one fluffy little dog. So I ring and explain I have large show dogs and they tend not to knock us back but we still ask to be put up the back away from people.'

She also recommends keeping your pets leashed in new surroundings as they almost lost a Lab once who bolted at the sound of a loudly opening door.

When they are not heading to shows, Fisher visits Moore Park caravan park in Queensland on the coast out from Bundaberg, which is very dog-friendly with great beach access.

'But I am constantly frustrated by how many people leave their dog's mess behind,' she says. 'There will come a time when these places that are dog-friendly change back to being unwelcoming to dogs if people don't clean up their mess.'

CHAPTER FOUR

CARAVANNING AND CAMPING

Swag the dog: the best places to pitch a tent or park the caravan with your canine companion

Campgrounds have long been the most dog-friendly option for people who want to take their pet around Australia. Though not all campgrounds are pet-friendly, there will be a much higher percentage of parks that will take dogs than, say, motels or hotels, so they are a safe bet if you don't want to spend too much time planning your accommodation.

That said, you still need to do some research. Make sure you check if there are requirements for your dog to be leashed, which is often the case if it is one of the rare campsites situated within a national park.

You should also ask the park operator if there is any additional cost to have your dog stay at the park, or if they require a bond, as some places do put extra charges on for cleaning. You might also need to check if there is a size limit on pets, or if there is a limit to the number of dogs that are allowed on one site if you own multiple pets.

A common size is 10 kilograms as an upper limit, which makes it trickier for larger or even just more solidly built dogs, though it is usually an arbitrary limit so it can still be worth calling ahead to check. We spoke to one dog owner who travels with a host of larger dogs but when she mentions she is heading to compete in a local agricultural show she is rarely knocked back as it is assumed the dogs are going to be well behaved.

Some parks may have 'pets on application' on their website or brochure, and this is really just another way for owners to reserve the right to say no if they don't like the sound of your pet or are not keen on particular breeds. Don't let this put you off either, most places really just want to be convinced that your dog is not going to annoy the other campers. You might even want to request a campsite that is in a corner spot, or away from common areas, so that you can help minimise any likelihood of your dog upsetting any non-dog lover who might be staying nearby.

Also be mindful that it's common for fox or wild-dog bait to be set in bushland areas. You can check with the local council for the area you are visiting to determine if this may be a risk, and reconsider your visit, keep your dog on a lead if this risk is present, or make sure that your dog is muzzled when it is not in your direct line of sight.

What follows are some of the most recommended parks and campsites for people who are travelling with their beloved pets. There are thousands of parks around the country but these caravan parks and campsites continue to pop up in online forums and in the discussions we have had for this book as places that are just that extra bit dog-friendly, which can make the difference between a good holiday and a great one.

Australian Capital Territory/New South Wales

Big 4, Batemans Bay

This site comes recommended for its camping as well as its onsite cabins that are pet-friendly. All pets need to be declared when booking a site/cabin. Reception staff will advise guests travelling with pets about the pet-friendly policy upon arrival, and there is also a $100 pet bond that is required when staying in the pet-friendly cabins.
big4.com.au

Belmont Caravan Park, Belmont

Experience the breathtaking views and relaxing island-like atmosphere at this unique caravan park that is almost completely encircled by the lake. Boat-hire facilities and safe launching ramps are all in close proximity and for those that prefer the ocean, the area's most stunning patrolled surfing and swimming beaches are just around the corner.
lakemacholidayparks.com.au

Wooyung Beach Holiday Park, Byron Bay

Wooyung, about 20 minutes north of Byron Bay, is best known as the location of the annual Splendour in the Grass music festival. The dog-friendly beach is right at your doorstep at this bush camping site and you can enjoy the smell and sounds of the beach and the ocean. The park is full of wildlife including water dragons and dozens of different types of birds.

Pets must be kept on lead and quiet at all times in the park and are not permitted in the cabins. Note that the park books out very quickly when the festival is on and over the Christmas holiday period.
wooyungbeach.com.au

Ingenia Holidays Byron Bay

Located just five-minutes' drive from the centre of Byron Bay, this is the largest accommodation provider in Byron Bay with a range of different spaces and accommodation styles. You're close enough to everything that Byron Bay has to offer but away from the hustle and bustle of the town.

The site is set in 28 acres of parklands, so keep an eye out for wildlife including koalas, echidnas and birds, and it fronts onto the dog-friendly Tallow Beach.

Pet-friendly sites and cabins are subject to availability, blackout dates and charges may apply. Contact the park directly to book.
www.ingeniaholidays.com.au/byron-bay

Cowra Holiday Park, Cowra
Recommended for the large amount of grassy areas on offer in the park and a big, unfenced area at the rear where dogs can go for a good supervised run. The park, which caters to caravanners, campers and those seeking self-contained accommodation, offers a range of accommodation including deluxe and standard self-contained one- and two-bedroom cabins, powered and unpowered sites, ensuite powered sites and a bunkhouse room.
cowraholidaypark.com.au

Glenmack Park, Kangaroo Valley
Recommended for families with pets as it is very animal-friendly, come and say hello to the park pets Harvey the horse, Mikey the pony, Ben and Jerry the twin miniature goats, Bambi, Yoda and Chewy the alpacas and Sir Rams-a-lot the sheep. Located in the heart of the stunning Kangaroo Valley beside the Kangaroo River, Glenmack Park offers picturesque mountain views in all directions and is landscaped to enhance the view.
glenmack.com.au

Parkes Country Cabins, Parkes
The cabins are located on Peak Hill Road, more commonly known as the Newell Highway, approximately two kilometres north of the Parkes city centre. It offers 35 air-conditioned cabins and a large camp kitchen available to use during your stay that has free barbecues, free pizza oven, drinks machine, a large screen TV and a table tennis table.
parkescountrycabins.com.au

Reflections, Hawks Nest

Dogs are permitted at Hawks Nest Holiday Park at selected sites and cabins year-round. But certain conditions do apply and the dogs are subject to park manager's discretion – so this is one where it is best to call the park directly to book. That said, many dog-trippers report a beautiful beachside location and great amenities.

reflectionsholidayparks.com.au

Reflections, Pambula

When the Reflections group are dog-friendly they go the extra mile, with Pambula even having a dog bath. One of the beaches at Pambula is off-lead all day but the beach at Mystery Bay is time share (no dogs between 9 am and 5 pm) in the peak season. Dogs on leads are allowed in all areas of the park except inside amenities and the camp kitchen. Dog waste stations are available onsite and in the adjoining reserve, so they are well set up for pooch visitors.

reflectionsholidayparks.com.au

Wee Jasper Reserve, Wee Jasper

A great spot to base yourself if you are exploring Canberra and surrounds, the park is set in the greenery of the farmland on the way to Yass (which is also worth a visit, drop in at the local wine bar Yazzbar; yazzbar.com.au). There are plenty of walks surrounding the park and you can move around to a variety of free camping in the area including Micalong Creek, Billy Grace camp, Carey's camp, Fitzpatrick Trackhead and Swinging Bridge.

weejasperreserves.com.au

Northern Territory

Heritage Caravan Park, Alice Springs

Set on around 10 acres just near Alice, this park has plenty of shady sites for caravanners as well as self-contained cabins. For the campers there is a bush camping area that runs to over 5 acres surrounded by lemon-scented gums. The Heritage Caravan Park offers pet-friendly

accommodation, a dedicated off-lead dog run and a K9000 dog wash, making it a genuinely pet-friendly park.
heritagecaravanpark.com.au

Batchelor Holiday Park, Batchelor
Also a good base for visiting Litchfield National Park, this park offers dog-friendly options and is recommended for the warmth of the owner's welcome and their care in looking after four-legged visitors. Batchelor Holiday Park is located just 14 kilometres from the boundary of the national park.
batchelorholidaypark.com.au

Bungle Bungle Caravan Park
This park comes highly recommended, with such a high level of dog friendliness they have minded dogs for people while they drove through the famous nearby mountain ranges – but check ahead for availability, as this is an off-menu service. The park even has luxe safari tents with and without ensuites that also welcome dogs.
bunglebunglecaravanpark.com.au

Lazy Lizard Tavern and Caravan Park, Pine Creek
The Lazy Lizard Tavern is a unique outback tavern. It is constructed from termite-mound mudbrick, and local ironwood featuring beautifully carved images of the local wildlife. The Lazy Lizard is in the heart of historic Pine Creek and offers both camp and caravan sites that allows you to bring your pets with you.
lazylizardpinecreek.com.au

Noonamah Tourist Park, Noonamah
Noonamah is around 40 minutes south of Darwin, just off the Stuart Highway. They have powered and unpowered sites as well as onsite cabins and the whole place is very pet-friendly.
noonamahtouristpark.com.au

Rum Jungle Bungalows, Rum Jungle
The camping and caravan sites are the dog-friendly accommodation options here. Dogs are not permitted in the cabins or other communal

areas and of course they are not permitted into Litchfield National Park, which is famous for the Lost City, an incredible collection of eroded rock that is only accessible by four-wheel drive.
rumjunglebungalows.com.au

Queensland

Coleyville Lodge Camping, Coleyville

Based on a working cattle farm, dogs are very welcome here, as are a host of other animals (including horses!). Located in the Scenic Rim about an hour from Brisbane, the handful of camp sites are mainly spread out along the far reaches of the property's waterholes, which are great for swimming, and each site has its own fire pit. Be sure to check the website before visiting though, as the property has been closed due to COVID-19 and adverse weather conditions.
mustdobrisbane.com

Fishermans Beach Holiday Park, Emu Park

They take bigger rigs at this park, which is recommended for some of the dog-friendly sites that are only 90 paces to the beach that is also off-lead. Fishermans Beach Holiday Park is located right on the beach in the village of Emu Park. Only a short stroll from cafes, the supermarket and heated public pool, Emu Park is on the doorstep of the Keppel Bay Islands and Capricorn Coast.
fishermansbeachhp.com.au

Tannum Sands Holiday and Caravan Park, Gladstone

Along the southern Great Barrier Reef, Tannum Sands is an oasis with multicoloured sunsets and year-round warm climes. For holidaymakers searching for true relaxation, the Gladstone region is the place to unwind. Check ahead as dogs are only permitted at certain cabins and sites.
discoveryholidayparks.com.au

Goomburra Valley Campground, Goomburra

Located on the Darling Downs and situated on the banks of Dalrymple Creek, the park has flat, shady areas for camping. They have powered

campsites available, most with a fire pit right next to the site. Well-behaved pets are welcome but ring ahead and check about the park's pet policy.
goomburravalleycampground.com.au

Windmill Caravan Park, Hervey Bay

Family owned, boutique-sized caravan park walking distance to pet-friendly beach and all the local attractions. All caravan and camp sites are pet-friendly as are two cabins and there is even a dog wash!
windmillpark.com.au

Bonus Downs Farmstay, Mitchell

This is a stay for the historical nuts as the homestead on this sprawling, beautifully restored property was first built in 1911 by one of Australia's most well-known landholders, Sir Samuel McCaughey. Caravans, camping and RVs are all welcome and accommodation is also available in historical jackaroos' quarters or the shearers shed.
mitchellqld.com

Moore Park Beach Holiday Park

An absolute beachfront location surrounded by parklands, 18 kilometres north of Bundaberg. Moore Park Beach boasts almost 20 kilometres of golden sandy beach and is also a nesting site for sea turtles, including loggerhead sea turtles, in summer months. The holiday park has waterfront powered and unpowered sites and fully self-contained cabins. Pets are welcome on application with current vaccination certificates.

Mt Larcom Tourist Park, Mt Larcom

This park comes recommended for those wanting to explore the Mt Larcom and the Gladstone region as dogs are welcome at the camp sites and inside the cabins (with prior approval). The park is set on 6.5 acres and has plenty of space for larger vans on powered and unpowered sites throughout the park.
mtlarcomtouristpark.com

Bigriggen Park, Rathdowney

Recommended for its family-friendly approach as well as being fur-family-friendly, Bigriggen Camping and Caravan Park is located in the Scenic

Rim, approximately 90 minutes from Brisbane and Gold Coast. The park is set in 100 acres of bushland and river flats surrounded by national parks and bordered by the Logan River and Burnett Creek.
bigriggen.com.au

South Australia

Riverbend Caravan Park, Renmark

The might Murray River is right at the doorstep of this park that features cabins and camp sites and plenty of in-park facilities. Dogs are welcome at the powered sites and in two of the cabins, both of which have a secure fenced-off area for dogs. Check the pet policy on the website for restrictions.
riverbendrenmark.com.au

Brighton Beachfront Holiday Park, Kingston Park

Located not far from Glenelg in Adelaide, it is all about the beach life here at Brighton, a well-recommended spot for (smaller) sand-loving pets with plenty of family-friendly facilities. Explore the many coastal reserve trails surrounding the property and the rich history of the area. Take the coastal walking track to historic Glenelg, the birthplace of South Australia, for a spot of shopping or visit the Seacliff Surf Club or Seacliff Beach Hotel for a meal.
brightonholidaypark.com.au

Pine Country Caravan Park, Mt Gambier

The pet-friendly accommodation here has all you'll need to ensure a comfortable stay with your four-legged friend. There is a mix of cabins and camping available for dog owners and you can hire a fire pit. The cabins are really well appointed for pets with kennels, a fenced yard and waters bowls and there is an off-lead dog paddock. Ask about doggy day care as it has been provided in the past.
pinecountry.com.au

Paringa Caravan Park, Paringa

Located in a beautiful bush setting 4 kilometres from Renmark, this park has been around since the 1970s and still has an old-world charm to it.

The park is pet-friendly and set on 2.6 acres with plenty of room to exercise you dog. Ask Tony and Jenni if you need some pet sitting and they might have some ideas too as they go the extra mile for guests.
paringacaravanpark.com.au

Port Vincent Foreshore Caravan Park, Port Vincent

This park is in a unique position on Surveyor Point, giving access on one side to a beach that is excellent for swimming and other aquatic activities, and with the other side perfect for fishing, crabbing and birdlife observations. The park is an easy two-hour drive from Adelaide and features all types of accommodation from luxury two-bedroom fully self-contained beachfront cabins to a range of powered sites with individual water connection. Check with the park about their pet policy before visiting as dogs may not be permitted during peak periods.
portvincentfcp.com.au

Almerta Station, Yanyarrie

Almerta Station is a family-owned property in the Flinders Ranges. The property is situated on the Boolcunda Creek around 20 kilometres north of Carrieton, three and half hours north of Adelaide. The station stretches from the Carrieton–Quorn Road to the peaks of the Mount James Ranges. Recommended for the 13 remote campsites where you can feel like you have the whole station to yourself.
almertastation.com.au

Tasmania

Allports Campsite, Flinders Island

The Allports campsite is just a hundred metres from the beach with track access to the sand, and there is a barbecue and table, though the area is basically free camping and you'll need to pack your own water and firewood. The site is 20 kilometres north of Whitemark, near the small settlement of Emita and close to Wybalena Chapel and Lillies Bay Campground.
flindersisland.net

Mole Creek Caravan Park, Mole Creek

Mole Creek, about an hour from Devonport, gets its name because the body of water digs itself underground in several places and you can tour the nearby Marakoopa Cave to see the underground river. The caves are home to the Tasmanian cave spider, a dinner-plate-sized, prehistoric arachnid. The caravan park is intimate and set around a bend in the creek said to hold a platypus. The powered site comes with a fire pit and the park has a large supply of firewood that only costs you a bit of effort, as you borrow the camp saw and cut the lumber to size. Dogs are welcome at the campsite but must be on a lead.
molecreek.net.au

Humbug Point, St Helens

Humbug Point Nature Recreation Area offers a large area for camping and caravans with easy access to Georges Bay. An excellent family holiday spot, the reserve is popular for birdwatching, walks, fishing and water activities, and there are plenty of great sites for rock and beach fishing and swimming.
parks.tas.gov.au

NRMA St Helens Waterfront Holiday Park

Overlooking the stunning Georges Bay on the north-east coast of Tasmania, NRMA St Helens Waterfront Holiday Park is just minutes from the Bay of Fires. Just a two-hour drive from Launceston, St Helens is known for having the warmest climate in Tasmania. Pet bookings are at the manager's discretion, and you must book directly with the park as they cannot be made online.

Quite a few NRMA parks do accept pets but it is important to note that some parks only offer it on a seasonal basis so be sure to call ahead and check.
nrmaparksandresorts.com.au

BIG4, Ulverstone

BIG4 Ulverstone Holiday Park offers a variety of accommodation choices in an award-winning caravan park, located directly opposite the beach and just 15 minutes to the *Spirit of Tasmania* Devonport terminal, making it the perfect place to base yourself while exploring the scenic Cradle Mountain, Leven Canyon, Penguin, Burnie, Devonport, Sheffield and the seaside town of Stanley.
big4.com.au

Victoria

Marengo Caravan Park, Apollo Bay

Recommended by many dog lovers who want to explore the Great Ocean Road, this park enjoys full beach frontage and is adjacent to the Marengo Reef Marine Sanctuary with its resident seal colony. The park is an ideal base for swimming, diving and snorkelling. Situated at the beginning of the Great Ocean Walk the park offers plenty of bushwalking trails and chances for a dip with your pup.

marengo-caravanpark.com.au

Big4 Ballarat Windmill Holiday Park

There is one dog-friendly cabin and four dog-friendly caravan and camping sites. Bookings are essential and you'll need to contact the park directly. The park has new fenced areas where you can back your caravan into the area, slide a door shut and park your mobile home inside your very own dog park. This way you can simply open the door and let your dog out to go to the toilet, or relax next to the van with a coffee. There are also plans to build a dog run.

ballaratwindmill.com.au

Beechworth Lake Sambell Caravan Park, Beechworth

This is a mix of dog-friendly sites and onsite cabins, with a pair of friendly pups featuring prominently on the park's website, which is always a good sign. The park is within easy reach of the Murray to Mountains Rail Trail and many walking tracks for you and your pet to explore.

caravanparkbeechworth.com.au

Wakiti Creek Resort, Echuca

Wakiti Creek Resort is a picturesque, secluded holiday park on over 60 acres of beautiful natural bushland on the banks of the Wakiti Creek. Situated just 30 minutes from the historical township of Echuca the park is also central to Barmah, Kyabram, Cobram, Shepparton, Tongala and all the tourist attractions on offer. The park has creek access for doggy dipping and a walking track through the bush where your pooch

can stretch their legs. The duplex cabins have a fenced courtyard at the front.
wakiticreekresort.com.au

Jerusalem Creek Campground, Eildon

The eight separate camping areas, situated on the southern tip of the Jerusalem Block, are a perfect base for exploring Lake Eildon National Park. Sites must be booked on a first-come, first-served basis and dogs are allowed on-lead. Make the most of the waterside location at Jerusalem Creek. Go swimming or launch a canoe, kayak or boat from the nearby boat ramp to explore further afield.
parks.vic.gov.au

Paradise Valley Camping Ground, Glenmaggie

Located on the banks of the Macalister River, Paradise Valley is a family camping park set on 60 acres with 1.5 kilometres of river frontage. The grassed campsites are free range and able to cater for single families, large group bookings or anything in between. There are 12 powered sites, three cabins and many unpowered sites.
paradisevalley.com.au

Johanna Beach Campground, Johanna

Located between coastal sand dunes, a lush grassy hinterland and a prime surf beach, the dog-on-lead friendly Johanna Beach Campground has everything you need for an unforgettable seaside camping experience. Johanna Beach Campground has 25 sites and there are non-flush toilets and no showers. You will need to bring your own drinking water.
parks.vic.gov.au

Prime Tourist Park, Lakes Entrance

There are doggy pictures all over the website of this very pet-friendly place and their dog-friendly accommodation does book out quite quickly so call ahead. The name of the park stems from its 'prime' location that is just a few hundred metres from the centre of Lakes Entrance, where you can buy prawns straight off the boat or wander

along the foreshore and watch fishermen feed the local pelicans their flathead offcuts. The park is very quiet at night as it is set back off the main road.
primetouristpark.com.au

Great Ocean Road Tourist Park, Peterborough
Recommended not only for its pet-friendliness but because there is an off-lead beach across the road from it. Caravanners and campers are well catered for with grassy, wind-protected sites and some of the sites even have river frontage.
greatoceanroadtouristpark.com.au

Western Australia

Wooramel River Station, Carnarvon
Wooramel Station is a family-owned working cattle, sheep and goat outback station. Located 120 kilometres south of Carnarvon on the Coral Coast, camp under the gumtrees on the Wooramel River with large shady or grassed sites with fire pits. Experience the naturally heated therapeutic artesian bore baths at this unique station property.
wooramel.com.au

Warroora Station, Carnarvon
Warroora is a family-run cattle station, an hour south of Coral Bay and 23 kilometres from the highway on a gravel road. The Homestead Campground with unpowered sites is 1.5 kilometres from the beach. The Homestead is accessible with 2WD but a 4WD vehicle is required to access the beach.

The area is spacious with lots of wildlife running around, including kangaroos and goannas as well as cattle. While the place is very clearly pet-friendly, the owners are clear that they do need to be well behaved, kept on a lead and cleaned up after. Note that baits are used on other parts of the property.
warroora.com

RAC Monkey Mia Dolphin Resort, Denham

This large and recently refurbished park with loads of facilities and amenities for all the family has a range of accommodation types but only the camp (powered and unpowered) and caravan sites are dog-friendly. The beachfront accommodation is located right on the shores of Shark Bay.

parksandresorts.rac.com.au/monkey-mia

Southern Stars Holiday Park, Dunsborough

Southern Stars Holiday parks claims to be the only holiday park in the south-west that not only allows guests to bring their dog but encourages it! There are powered sites, unpowered sites, sites for big rigs, and even fully fenced sites so your dog can enjoy some time off-lead.

southernstarspark.com.au

Bullara Station, Exmouth Gulf

The Shallcross family have owned the station since the 1950s, and there is a range of accommodation options from camping and glamping to an old shearers lodge that can sleep 16. The spacious bush camp area (perfect for caravans and tents) has powered and unpowered sites with communal fire pits and unique showers and toilets. All the sites are surrounded by stunning scenery and native wildlife, delivered with rustic charm and first-class country hospitality.

bullarastation.com.au

Banksia Tourist Park, Hazelmere

The park is situated in some beautiful country at the base of the Perth Hills, the sites are spacious and there is doggy daycare available. The off-lead Greenslopes Dog Park is a short stroll from the park, too.

banksiatourist.com.au

Logue Brook Campground, Hoffman

Part of Lake Brockman, Logue Brook Dam is a designated water ski area and there is a boat-launching area adjacent to the campground. This park is surrounded by state forest with 126 powered and unpowered

sites, which can accommodate large RVs, and has plenty of amenities. There are two pump tracks suitable for mountain-bike riders of all abilities and fitness levels at the campground and the Munda Biddi trail passes nearby.
parks.dpaw.wa.gov.au

Marrinup Townsite Campground, Holyoake
There are around a hundred camp sites at this campground, not far from the city of Perth. The site is home to the Marrinup walk and cycle trail, or the hardcore can take on the much longer Munda Biddi mountain bike trail. Sites can't be pre-booked and you will need to bring drinking water with you.
parks.dpaw.wa.gov.au

Anchorage Caravan Park, Kalbarri
On the banks of the Murchison River and in the centre of town, the park offers powered and unpowered sites as well as cabins. Pet-friendly outside school holidays for van and tent sites only (a $30 bond applies to sites booked with pets).
kalbarri.org.au

Nanga Mill Campground, Nanga Brook
Built on the site of an historic jarrah sawmill, Nanga Mill is now a campground with space for 55 large tents, camper trailers or caravans and there are plenty of pet-friendly options. If you are up for some 4WD action there are plenty of tracks nearby, and the Murray River is within walking distance.
parks.dpaw.wa.gov.au

Perth Central Caravan Park
The Perth Central Caravan Park in Ascot is the closest holiday park to the centre of Perth, with plenty of dog-friendly sites and cabins on offer. The park is located in between the Perth Airport and the city and is just a three-minute walk from the Swan River. There are great amenities, including a huge outdoor kitchen and large swimming pool. If you need

to take your dog for a walk the nearby Ayres Bushland, Garvey Park or Claughton Reserve are great spots for your pup to relieve a bad case of the zoomies.

perthcentral.com.au

Pinjarrah Holiday Park, Pinjarra

Situated on farmland, the Pinjarrah Holiday Park offers 70 dog-friendly grass sites and plenty of amenities for campers. Campfires are allowed in season provided an enclosed fire container is used. Wood should be brought with you or purchased locally. There are 100 acres of the property that act as an off-lead area for dogs so if you have an active breed then this is the spot for you.

pinjarrahholidaypark.com.au

Red Bluff Camping & Caravan, Red Bluff

Located at the southern end of the Ningaloo Marine Park, the whole camp overlooks the Indian Ocean, and is on the path of the annual pilgrimage of humpback whales, from late May–October.

Dogs are permitted by arrangement out the front of the homestead and north of the homestead and on a limited part of the beach (1080 baits are used on other parts of the property). Dogs are welcome as long as rules are adhered to and $50 dog bond applies.

While there is a shop with basic camping supplies that is open in season, visitors need to ensure they have sufficient fuel, water and food for their stay. The closest services are located in Carnarvon (125 kilometres south).

quobba.com.au

Sues Bridge Camping Ground, Blackwood River National Park

Sues Bridge has an undercover camp kitchen with gas barbecues, cold water taps (using collected rainwater), dishwashing sinks, food preparation surfaces and picnic tables and benches. There is access to the Blackwood River for swimming and to launch canoes and kayaks.

The campground, and the whole of the South West Capes area, is very popular during school holidays and weekends from October to April, particularly public holiday weekends. Be prepared with an alternative place to stay at these times in case there is no suitable site available.

TRAVEL TAILS

Anastasia Elizabee and Oscar the Tibetan spaniel, New South Wales

Anastasia Elizabee went on a three-month adventure with her Tibetan spaniel Oscar, from Michelago in New South Wales to Cape Tribulation in Queensland and back again, covering some serious miles. She found that Far North Queensland was pretty dog-friendly despite the large number of national parks and marine reserves, but she felt that a lot of places were more used to seeing working dogs than dogs like her spoiled boy Oscar!

She stayed mostly in motels and found that there was a big difference between places tagged as pet-friendly and those that really loved having dogs stay at their premises.

'These were the ones that would welcome the dogs as well as you. They were people who were used to living with dogs and they would have water sitting outside reception,' she says. 'In these places having your dog was not a fuss, whereas one place we had to pay extra and I am pretty sure that was not in the rental agreement.'

She found that the pet filter on Booking.com was a bit hit and miss but still found some great places to stay, as well as some great doggy daycare so she was free to do some exploring.

'If I was going to take a trip, like I went to the aquarium in Townsville, I found doggy daycare,' Elizabee says. 'And he ended up not even wanting to come home with me afterwards he was having such a good time. He had his paw prints done and a picture of him and he was assessed for his personality traits, it was just amazing.'

That place was Dogtopia in Townsville (dogtopiaretreat.com.au) but she also recommends a stay at Floriana Villas in Cairns,

Canberra Pet Care in Wickerslack near Canberra (canberrapetcare.com.au), Country Plaza Motor Inn in Mackay (countryplaza.com.au) and the Chalet Motor Inn in Bundaberg (chaletmotorinn.com.au) where she was welcomed by the pair of in-house pugs. She was also a fan of Lync Haven Rainforest Retreat near the Daintree (lynchaven.com.au), Ingenia Holidays, Broulee (ingeniaholidays.com.au) and the Tully Motel in Tully (tullymotel.com.au).

CHAPTER FIVE

MOTELS

Let sleeping dogs lie: motels for the road-tripping doggo

When you are on a road trip there is a great appeal in being able to just drive up to the front door of your accommodation, get out of the car, lock the door and crash out for the night; then slip out in the morning with the key left dangling in the front door. Motels are a road-tripper's dream; an easy, clean and no-nonsense way for you to catch a good night's sleep without deviating too far from your chosen path. Also, motel biscuits are amazing.

But all motels are not created equal: there is a lot of variety in quality and service and not all of them welcome pets in their rooms.

But at Jugiong Motor Inn (jugiongmotorinn.webs.com), at the gateway to the Hilltops Region in New South Wales, Jen and Mark Milner have a whole dog-friendly wing to their charming motel set in a huge acreage just off the Hume Highway. There is a huge amount of grass where the dogs can run around and the motor inn is just a short walk from the Murrumbidgee River, where you can take a stroll or throw in a fishing line. When the pair first took on the accommodation it was very far from the pet-friendly place it is today, but that was one of the first changes they made to put their stamp on the place.

'When we first came here every room had a huge sign saying "If you have a dog in your room you will be asked to leave with no refund of your money" and we thought that was quite severe,' Jen says. 'But we have dogs ourselves, and now if you are travelling with a bird or a dog you are welcome to have pets in the rooms.'

The motor inn prefers pets to have their own bed and there is a small surcharge for cleaning but it makes sense to the couple to offer the service because, as pet owners themselves, they know how people treat their dogs as part of the family.

Jen says that when you allow animals in a room you expect a certain level of respect and that '99 per cent of people give you that'.

To that end, Jen has some simple advice for those bringing their pets to a motel. 'If you are travelling with your dog, always pick up after it.

If it does make a mess in the room just clean it up. Make it nice for the person who is offering the accommodation because, if you are nice to people who are offering pet-friendly accommodation, the more likely they will be to stay pet-friendly.'

Jugiong Motor Inn does divide the motel into pet-friendly rooms and non-pet-friendly, in respect to those travellers with allergies. The motor inn has a bar and restaurant on premises that is popular with the locals so you don't have to head anywhere else for dinner – though the neighbouring Long Track Pantry makes one of the best bacon-and-egg rolls on the whole Hume Highway, if not Australia, so stop there for breakfast when you leave. On chilly evenings you can sit outside with your dog around the old pot-bellied stove and swap stories with other pet-friendly road trippers.

And if you are up early enough you will see Jen and Mark serving breakfast to the rest of the Jugiong Motor Inn family in the paddock nearby; a crew that includes sheep, cows, alpacas and Poppy the 300-kilogram pig. Watching Poppy amble towards you is a sight that neither you, nor your pup, will soon forget.

Below is our round-up of some of the best dog-friendly motels around the country.

Australian Capital Territory/New South Wales

Major Mitchell Motel, Bourke

Located just a few minutes' walk from the beautiful Darling River, this low-key motel on a quiet, tree-lined street is close to the supermarket, shops and the club and pub.

majormitchellmotel.com.au

Desert Sand Motor Inn, Broken Hill

The motel was originally built in 1973 and prior to that the land served as stables as part of the Southern Cross Hotel built in 1888. The hotel served as a coach station around the turn of the century, where the passengers could refresh and the horses could rest. It has a bar, pool and barbecue area, and there is a restaurant right next door.

desertsand.com.au

Warrumbungles Mountain Motel, Coonabarabran

Located 9 kilometres west of Coonabarabran in a picturesque valley, bordered on three sides by the Castlereagh River this is the closest accommodation to the Warrumbungle National Park and Peter Starr's Warrumbungle Observatory. There are barbecues, a pool and guest laundry.
warrumbungle.com

Eden Motel, Eden

The motel is situated in the heart of beautiful Eden on the Sapphire Coast of New South Wales, the most southerly town in the state. The property is only minutes from clubs, pubs, shops, golf club and the Lake Curalo Boardwalk, an easy, flat walk that circles the entire lake and joins with the Aslings Beach Maritime Walk. It is a great option for exercising your dog and there is a great off-lead dog beach just 400 metres away.
edenmotel.com

Jolly Swagman Motor Inn, Holbrook

This small older-style motel with friendly staff and clean, comfortable rooms is a convenient dog-friendly stop just off the highway between Sydney and Melbourne. There are grassy areas around the motel where your dog can stretch their legs and take care of business. Contact the motel directly to book your pet-friendly room.
holbrookmotelgroup.com.au

Jugiong Motor Inn, Jugiong

See profile in introduction.
jugiongmotorinn.webs.com

Buccaneer Motel, Long Jetty

Buccaneer Motel Long Jetty is just a short distance from The Entrance waterfront. The famous pelican feeding is at 3:30 pm every day. Check it out but keep your pooch on a lead.
buccaneermotel.com.au

Leagues Motel, Queanbeyan

The Leagues Motel in Queanbeyan overlooks the peaceful Molonglo River. This motel has studio rooms and apartments with varying bedding

configurations and is just a couple of minutes' walk to the centre of town. Queanbeyan is convenient and central for all Canberra's best tourist attractions and businesses in and around the Capital Country.
leaguesmotel.net

Grand Manor Motor Inn, Queanbeyan East
Slanted towards the business traveller but great for a pet-friendly family stay too, the Grand Manor offers twin share and deluxe queen rooms and the Grand Manor family room. The onsite Mind Your Manors restaurant serves up motel staples like schnitzels, burgers and fish and chips if you don't want to travel too far for dinner.
grandmanor.net.au

Northern Territory

Katherine Motel, Katherine
Located in the heart of Katherine, this is the perfect place to stay if you want clean, comfortable and relaxing accommodation that's close to all the action. The Katherine Motel is situated just 30 metres away from the main street in Katherine and they have a reputation for being very welcoming of guests with dogs.
katherinemotel.com

Eldorado Motor Inn, Tennant Creek
Located at the northern end of the Tennant Creek township, the Eldorado Motor Inn offers genuine outback hospitality with modern facilities. Take a dip in the refreshing pool, or just sit back and admire the amazing crystal-clear desert sky. Enjoy a fantastic buffet dinner, real Aussie barbecue or a la carte menu at the Eldorado licensed restaurant.
northernterritory.com

Queensland

Ocean View Motel, Bowen

Bowen is located on the north-east coast of Queensland, approximately 550 kilometres south of Cains. This beautiful old town has a lot of seaside activities to offer. The motel is on the southern approach to the town, right near the Big Mango, with views across the bay. There are dedicated pet-friendly rooms and a large, fully fenced pet exercise yard so your dog can have a run outdoors after a long drive. There is an onsite pool as well.
bowenoceanviewmotel.com.au

Dooley's Tavern & Motel, Capella

The Dooley family has warmly welcomed locals and travellers to this large motel for more than 75 years. Dooley's offers some of the best accommodation, food, service – and a little piece of Ireland – in the middle of the Bowen Basin/Central Highlands of Queensland. The onsite bar and bistro is open for lunch and dinner seven days a week.
dooleyscapella.com.au

Mid City Motor Inn, Mackay

This motel offers 34 comfortable and quiet rooms with views of the Pioneer River. Located one block from the centre of town, and just a short drive to the Whitsundays, this is a very conveniently located spot.
midcitymotel.com.au

Tin Can Bay Motel, Tin Can Bay

Just a short stroll from the Tin Can Bay waterfront, this motel has beautiful gardens, a pool and a barbecue and the whole place is pet-friendly. Just a few kilometres from the motel is Norman Point, which is well known for the dolphin feeding next to the boat ramp between 7 and 8.30 each morning, year-round.
tincanbaymotel.com.au

Shelly Beach Motel, Urangan

All rooms at the Shelly Beach Motel offer beautiful views of the tranquil

waters of Hervey Bay, either from the top-floor balconies or from the ground-floor courtyard. Wake up to the sun glinting on the waters of the bay, walk along the beach or take a morning tea or coffee with that fantastic view.
shellybeachmotel.com.au

South Australia

Highway One Motel, Ceduna

Highway One Motel is a 22-room motel situated on the Eyre Highway adjacent to the OTR Roadhouse. The motel offers standard or deluxe rooms, many with sea views, for those about to set off across the Nullarbor for the west, or just exploring South Australia.
facebook.com/highwayonemotel

Adelaide Road Motor Lodge, Murray Bridge

Adelaide Road Motor Lodge, situated just outside the town centre, offers both deluxe and economy accommodation and there is a large outdoor pool. The motel is a short drive from local cafes and restaurants and has a charge-back dinner arrangement with the award-winning Murray Bridge Hotel.
adelaiderdmotorlodge.com

Crossroads Ecomotel, Port Augusta

Crossroads Ecomotel was purpose built in 2014 and is the newest motel in Port Augusta. The energy-efficient buildings are built with internal rammed earth walls for thermal mass that keeps the rooms cool in summer and warm in winter.

This is a modern and pet-friendly option for travellers. Pets are not allowed on the beds or furniture, and there is a limit of one pet per booking (unless by prior arrangement with management).
ecomotel.com.au

Lakeview Motel, Robe

Lakeview Motel is located a short walk or drive from the centre of town and has views over Lake Fellmongery. It's also a short drive from Robe

Lighthouse and features free parking. The rooms are air conditioned, with cable TV with on-demand movies, and a minibar fridge.
lakeview-motel-and-apartments-robe.booked.net

Tasmania

City View Motel, Montagu Bay, Hobart

City View Motel, Hobart is located on Hobart's Eastern Shore with stunning views across the Derwent to the city centre. It's a unique, hidden gem with updated 1960s design and decor. A great place to stay with your pet in the Apple Isle.

The motel is located opposite Gordons Hill Reserve, so you can take your pooch out for a morning stroll, and there is more information on the motel's website about the best place to get out and about with your dog during your stay. Pet-friendly rooms are limited and are not available online, they must be booked with the property directly. Bring your dog's bed and bowl and you're good to go!

Junction Motel, New Norfolk

New Norfolk is an historic town located in the picturesque Derwent Valley north-west of Hobart. Use the cosy Junction Motel as your base to explore southern Tasmania. One of the most awarded motels in the region, the Junction has recently undergone extensive renovation and boasts that it is 'just two and a half hours to anywhere in Tasmania'.
junctionmotel.com.au

Beachway Motel, Ulverstone

This motel is set upon two idyllic acres, just a stone's throw from the scenic Buttons Beach, and a short walk from the centre of Ulverstone. It is also located in close proximity to dining, shopping, and scenic hotspots – the Beachway Motel really is an ideal base in Ulverstone.
beachwayulverstone.com.au

Waterfront Motel, Wynyard

Located on the Inglis River, this motel offers absolute waterfront accommodation with a retro vibe and is just minutes from Burnie,

centrally located on the north-west coast of Tassie. They have two pet-friendly rooms and prefer smaller to medium-sized pets (20 kilograms or less).
waterfrontwynyard.com

Victoria

Bairnsdale Motor Inn, Bairnsdale

This comfortable older-style motel offers great value for money and has an outdoor pool and plenty of parking for larger vehicles. There is free wifi and a fully licensed bar and restaurant onsite. For breakfast drop by Northern Ground (facebook.com/northerngroundfood) an art-bedecked alcove further down Bairnsdale's main drag that does amazing brunch.
bairnsdalemoterinn.com.au

Philadelphia Motor Inn, Echuca

This motel is a five-minute drive from the heart of Echuca and has 24 spacious ground floor rooms with spa rooms, family rooms, queen rooms, twin rooms and triple rooms. Experience the Murray River, a fantastic holiday destination, and enjoy room service with an extensive menu and selection of fine wines – an unusual and welcome addition to normal motel services.
philadelphiamotorinn.com.au

Echuca Gardens, Echuca

A quirkier take on a standard motel offering, you can choose between the heritage-designed gypsy wagons, one-bedroom apartment, two-bedroom apartment or the 150-year-old woodcutter's cottage. All options are surrounded by magnificent water gardens and on the edge of state forest within walking distance to the river, historic port and town centre. Pets are welcome in all units with prior approval and there is an enclosed yard.
echucagardens.com

River Country Inn, Moama

River Country Inn is five minutes' drive from the Port of Echuca and has 27 spacious rooms all on ground level, a saltwater swimming pool and free covered barbecue facilities. You can park right at your back door and your front door opens onto the tranquil gardens. There is one pet-friendly room available and you will need to show proof of current vaccinations.

Keep it in mind if you want to attend the popular Riverboats Music Festival (riverboatsmusic.com.au) which happens each year.

echucamoama.com/river-country-inn

Flinders Cove Motel, Mornington Peninsula

The small peaceful village of Flinders is set amidst some of the most spectacular scenery of the Mornington Peninsula and is an ideal base for touring the peninsula wineries, restaurants, Peninsula Hot Springs, arts and crafts, markets, surf beaches, golf courses and national parks. This older-style budget motel has spacious rooms and enclosed courtyards for your pooch. The trendy Georgie Bass cafe and cooking school is right next door.

flinderscovemotel.com.au

A1 Motels, Port Fairy

Enjoy the hospitality at this budget accommodation located just off the highway and a short walk from everything picturesque Port Fairy has to offer including the beach, wharf, restaurants and cafes, antique and craft shops. The rooms are spacious and there's a large grassy area.

portfairymotorinn.com.au

Advance Motel, Wangaratta

Perfect for families, couples, groups and individuals, Advance Motel Wangaratta provides ample parking for trailers and large vehicles, free wifi, pet-friendly accommodation and substantial group discounts. There are four suites reserved for pets (and owners), and these are the same as an Executive Queen Suite. Reservations must be made directly with the motel. Pet blankets are available free of charge.

advancemotel.com.au

Western Australia

Georgiana Molloy Motel, Augusta

The Georgiana Molloy Motel is in the historical district and minutes from Augusta Visitor Centre and Augusta Historical Museum. Augusta is located where the Indian and Southern oceans meet and the Blackwood River flows into the sea, in the beautiful south-west of WA. The 16 air-conditioned rooms feature kitchens and free wifi.
augustasmolloymotel.com.au

Kimberley Croc Motel, Kununurra

The crowning glory of Western Australia is the Kimberley region of northern Australia. In it lays Kununurra, the jewel in the crown. The Kimberley Croc Motel boasts a central location, good-priced accommodation and comfortable rooms. It is a tropical paradise set in lush surroundings, a place to refresh, replenish, rehydrate, and relax. They even have pet beds available.
kimberleycrocmotel.com.au

Travellers Rest Motel, Mundaring

This family-owned stay in the Mundaring Hills is just a 30-minute drive from Perth and is a country-style motel that has been a favourite with travellers for the past decade. Just near Mundaring's town centre, there is also plenty of bushwalking for you and your dog.
travellersrestwa.com.au

TRAVEL TAILS

Adrienne Louise and Max the Kelpie

When Louise finally got to pick up Max, after spending a long time during 2020 trying to find a puppy, she was very excited to take him up to see her family in Sydney. But she was also a little concerned about taking a long road trip with such a young puppy, unsure about how he would handle life on the road.

'I gave him plenty of time to settle in but when he was around four months I decided to take him up to see my mum,' Louise said. 'I was concerned how he would travel but this was also the first time I have travelled with a dog so I was also worried that the accommodation that allowed pets would be sub-standard and smell like dog.'

Louise decided to break up the journey with a stop each way. Her first taste of dog-friendly accommodation was the Jolly Swagman Motor Inn (holbrookmotelgroup.com.au) in the New South Wales town of Holbrook.

'It was a real surprise, clean, friendly and it had a fully enclosed dog run right beside the room so Max could go for a run and to the toilet in total safety just near my accommodation,' she said. 'I am crate training him, so I took that with me and to my surprise he slept straight through the night at the end of my bed. In the morning I got up and took him for a walk around the famous Holbrook submarine and got a French vanilla slice from the Holbrook bakery. A lot of country towns lay claim to the best vanilla slice in Australia, but my vote is definitely for Holbrook. That is one of the things I love about travelling with a dog, I would have just got up and left that town without stopping but Max needing a walk got me out and exploring the town.'

Louise says that Max was great in the car, provided he had a good walk before the long stretches of driving, and there was not a single accident from the young pup. 'I would say to anyone that wants to travel with their dogs of any age, I understand there is some anxiety – will they travel well, will they behave, get carsick, or will they sleep in foreign rooms – but seeing Max take to the road so easily you just have to give it a try. Dogs are really adaptable so don't let having a pet limit your travelling.'

After a week in Sydney, Max and Louise headed back to Melbourne with an overnight stay in Canberra.

'Canberra really is a very dog-friendly place with loads of outdoor activities around the lake and a lot of restaurants and breweries that will accept you and your dog,' she says. 'I really wanted to test out a hotel that takes dogs, as I'm not much of a camper, so we stayed in the Abode Narrabundah (abodehotels.com.au) and I was surprised by how nice, and how welcoming, they were. Having Max in a hotel room was initially weird but I love that these options are opening up to dog owners and I would stay there again.'

The trip back was equally uneventful ('Except for one close call where Max had to go to the toilet behind a freeway service station – they could use more grassed areas in some of these places.') and now Max is a road-tripping doggy.

CHAPTER SIX

HOLIDAY HOMES

Hair-bnb: Finding a pet-friendly holiday home

Whether your go-to rental website is Airbnb, Stayz, specific local networks or pet-friendly sites like Holiday Paws, there are a few things you should know before hiring a holiday home for you and your whole pawesome family.

Simone Scoppa is a travel expert at Stayz who has been with the company for four years as PR manager and knows a thing or two about the perfect pet-friendly holiday rental. She is also the owner of Instagram celeb Taco the cocker spaniel (@tacothecocker).

'Fun fact for you, one in four of the 55,000 homes that we have in Australia on Stayz are, in fact, pet-friendly,' Scoppa says. 'We get asked this all the time "Can I bring my dog?" We know, especially in the last year, that dog ownership has gone up so more people are taking their dogs with them and I have heard from holiday home owners across the country that they are being asked a lot more.'

Scoppa says more Stayz homes are being made dog-friendly, and not just allowing pets outside but inside as well, because people have worked out that a well-behaved dog really does not make a lot of mess. 'It is more the humans sometimes,' she laughs.

Scoppa travels with Taco a lot and has some tips for grabbing a holiday stay, both as a pet owner and knowing how Stayz works. The first thing is to use the pet-friendly filter so you do not waste time looking at places that won't house your pooch.

'Another thing is that it is helpful just to look at the house rules that the property owner has set. Some owners may still want your dog to be outside so it is not on the soft furnishing, so before booking just make sure you are looking at those house rules,' she says.

Scoppa says you should also check with the owner what sort of facilities they actually have for the dog if they are listed as pet-friendly. Don't assume that means that you don't have to bring anything with you.

'I use as an example a house down in Jervis Bay called Blueys Beach House and it won one of the best pet-friendly accommodations in Australia a couple of years ago in awards for Stayz,' Scoppa says. 'They even had dog bowls, toys for the dog, a bed for the dog to sleep in, so they really know that there are lots of travellers out there that want to bring their dogs and there are a lot of added benefits. As a dog owner, we know what it is like to jump in the car to go on a road trip, there is lots of junk you have in the car and if you don't have to put your dog bed and all these other things in then that is gold. It is sort of like having a baby – do you have a foldaway cot, do you have a highchair? – people are asking about doggy bowls and toys, and a fenced yard as well.'

Scoppa says this last one is important for many dog owners who might have a doggy that gets the wanders. Most properties will tell you, but if it is not on the site then make sure you ask the owners.

Space to unwind

The appeal of holiday homes for dog owners is that you have your own space, you are not sitting on top of each other, and you can relax. You know there is more space for the dog to run around and for dogs that live in the city they can have space to explore, get those zoomies out and experience life in the country.

'They might see a llama for the first time,' Scoppa says. 'We were at this property in Kangaroo Valley and Taco was "What the hell is that thing?" and the property owner was great because they had this really great fence so the dog was interacting with the farm animals, or not interacting with them but he could see them.'

Scoppa says that there are often other dogs on the property to play with, too. She recalls a property up in Bellingen on the Never Never River where Taco got to meet two dogs that came to play. Owners with pets usually introduce their dogs on the property as well so you can see 'a kind of dog-loving community happening'. She says that the more dog-friendly places are definitely regional, with more space for pups to play.

Putting on her dog-owner hat, travelling with the Insta-famous Taco has been great for Scoppa. She says there is a great dog community in the social networks and they often meet up with other cocker spaniels they have connected with online and swap tips of places to stay.

'We had gone up to Byron when Taco was about a year old,' she says, 'and messaged this lady that we knew was based in Byron Bay with her dog and we were like "Hi! I know you don't really know us but we are in Byron and we are taking Taco to the dog park. Do you live anywhere near here?" and she was like, "Oh my God I am absolutely coming". So we met her at the dog park and we went to the dog-friendly beach and got to hang out with her. It was like a weird first date situation but with a dog owner. But I thought that was cool that people are using Instagram to find other like-minded dog owners when they are going on holidays. And she had all the tips about dog-friendly places in the area.

'Having worked in travel for years it is nice that more and more people are taking their dogs with them and you can share those memories,' Scoppa says.

On the practical side of road tripping, Scoppa says it is important to get the drive itself right. 'I think the actual road trip makes a lot of dog owners anxious,' she says. 'For us it is having the right toys, and having his comfy bed on the back seat, having those breaks every two hours, as you should as a responsible driver. You know what though? I wish that more of those highway service centres had greater grass areas for dogs because sometimes you are in weird concreted areas.'

Scoppa brings familiar things from home and tries to replicate as much of Taco's routine as possible when they are at the holiday home. 'We went to Yamba recently with the family, had a holiday rental there, and we took his bed, put it in the same location at the end of our bed, had his water bowl in the kitchen where it normally is, so it is just having that familiarity.

'Dogs will soon take over and become the boss of that new house anyhow.'

We present below some of the top rated, and best recommended, houses on offer at the various accommodation websites. Jump on the website and use the pet filters to find an even wider range of options.

Australian Capital Territory

Lyttle Cook BnB, Canberra

The property is in a very handy area, close to bike paths that go to the city via the lake, or to the Westfield shopping centre, and bikes are also available for use. You are situated conveniently to the Australian Institute of Sport and Canberra Stadium, the very dog-friendly National Arboretum and the National Museum. The city is a 10-minute drive away, then over the bridge to the National Library, Questacon, the National Gallery of Australia and National Portrait Gallery, Old Parliament House and the 'big house on the hill'.

Samanda's, Canberra

Samanda's B&B is a beautiful modern and very glamorous one-bedroom apartment that offers all the comforts of a hotel and yet much more space and extras. Located in the Tuggeranong Valley and backing onto a nature reserve, Samanda's is the perfect choice for a couples retreat, business base or short- to medium-term stay.

Short Stays@Janine's, Canberra

This lovely four-bedroom house is in a very quiet and peaceful suburban street. Short Stays@Janine's offers comfortable clean and well-equipped accommodation for budget-conscious travellers. Whether you are visiting the national capital for work or leisure, friends or family, this is a great spot to base yourself. And you can head out and enjoy one of the most dog-friendly cities with plenty of dog parks, lake walks and places to visit.

Ainslie Pet Friendly Apartment, Canberra

This cosy, modern courtyard apartment is situated at the back of the owner's suburban property. The private entrance takes you into the combined lounge and dining area. The compact kitchen includes a Nespresso coffee machine. Wifi and Foxtel are included. A small pantry of food basics is also available for your convenience as well as some breakfast items.

Maison Executive, Canberra

Fully furnished, serviced private luxury villas in the heart of Canberra available for two-night stays, up to six months if you need a longer visit. Whether you're travelling for a business trip or recreation, stay in comfort. These stays are two-storey, three-bedroom, two-bathroom villas, each with study and private gardens for your pets. There is also double garage parking for your vehicle with internal access.

New South Wales

Ruby Tuesday, Anna Bay

Close to the beach, sand dunes and shops you will find everything you need at this beachside property. This single-level home has a central open-plan living area that captures that ocean breeze and is perfect for casual entertaining, as well as just hanging out with your pupper.

Genie House, Byron Bay

This pet-friendly guesthouse is just a short stroll from all the action in the centre of Byron Bay. It can sleep up to six people and has a fully enclosed grassy front yard so your furry friend can explore safely.

Dark Skies Cottage, Coonabarabran

Dark Skies is a self-contained oasis, located in the heart of town and in close proximity to all amenities, including restaurants, parks, pubs, shops and other points of interest. A place to relax and recharge in style, while enjoying everything that Coonabarabran has to offer.

Betty Beach House, Eden

Betty Beach House is a renovated cottage, practically on the beach in Eden. It has off-street parking for boat and cars and there is an enclosed, fully fenced back garden for kids and dogs (both are welcome!).

Blake Loft on Manning, Kiama

Tastefully decorated throughout, this two-bedroom loft has an open-plan living area that flows onto the verandahs and balcony. You can rest in the comfortable lounges, sit back and unwind. A well-equipped kitchen is there to create a platter for the afternoon refreshments on the balcony as the Jacaranda shifts in the coastal breeze. Pawfect relaxation.

Tinonee Cottages, Manning Valley

These two historic cottages are overlooking the Manning River and are incredibly peaceful. The Manor sleeps up to eight and is child- and pet-friendly (that doesn't really do it justice – they have the perfect set-up for kids and four-legged family members). The Cottage is for couples or singles only, but pets are still allowed.

Firefly Cottage, Mudgee

Firefly Cottage is a recently renovated three-bedroom semi-detached double-brick cottage, built in 1870, situated right in the middle of Mudgee. The stay is just a short stroll to shops, hotels, restaurants, clubs, gyms and parks. This quirky cottage has been tastefully decorated and is very comfortable. Sleeping up to eight adults, it is suitable for anything from a romantic weekend away to a family gathering, with your dog, of course.

Lighthouse View, Mullumbimby

Beautiful self-contained studio, adjacent to the main house, with its own private entrance and large deck located just an eight-minute drive from Mullumbimby. The house is set on 2 acres of amazing gardens with expansive views and you can watch the lighthouse from your bed at night. The property is located on a private road, in a lush area just outside Mullumbimby that winds up to the surrounding escarpment. The views are magnificent; both of the hinterland and overlooking Cape Byron.

The Big Beach Shack, New Brighton

The big beach shack is perfectly positioned for a seaside getaway. It is a perfect pet-friendly getaway located one street from a dog-friendly beach and the river. Kick back, listen to the sea in the spacious, private courtyard or walk to a Pilates class, massage and health services, all conveniently located in the nearby street.

Safety Beach Bungalows, Safety Beach

The bungalows are surrounded by tropical gardens, with amazing bird life and a local mob of visiting kangaroos. The property is just 2 kilometres north of Woolgoolga (near Coffs Harbour).

The Soul Haven, Shoalhaven Heads

Lovingly restored, this original Shoalhaven Heads beach shack has been brought back to life for a new generation of holidaymakers to enjoy. The new owners of The Soul Haven saw these fibro shacks as a unique piece of Australian and local history and undertook the restoration and transformation of this gorgeous house. The property is only two hours from Sydney and three from Canberra.

Calm Waters Waterfront Cottages, Sussex Inlet

The six two- and three-bedroom cottages with different bedding configurations, are set up around a garden with river frontage and timber decking overlooking the water. Book ahead as they are very popular with dog travellers on Facebook groups.

Home Away From Home, Tamworth

Completely renovated just 12 months ago, the kitchen is the heart of this holiday home and a space you will certainly enjoy throughout your stay. The two front rooms accommodate two guests each, with the room at the rear of the house having two single beds to accommodate the kids. Fido can sleep where he likes.

Tathra Cottage, Tathra

Located about 100 metres east of the Tathra Homestead, Tathra Cottage is a cosy, mud-brick cottage with cathedral ceilings that offers a rustic farmstay experience for city dogs.

There is a secure area for your dog within the grounds and under the cottage roofline to provide guests with somewhere secure to leave their dog when visiting attractions in the local area. Guests must make sure their dogs are under control on the grounds as there are ducks, geese and chickens that free-range their way around the property.

Ocean Paws, Terrigal

Ocean Paws is a Terrigal Beach property that is immaculately maintained and is the perfect spot for beach-loving dogs. This modern style cabin is set on a beautiful half-acre property, making it perfect as a couples retreat or friends getaway. Pets are very welcome here.

Elm Cottage, Tumut

Elm Cottage has five luxurious cottages to choose from at this farm stay located by the Goobarragandra River just 14 kilometres east of Tumut. The property has stunning river and valley views and the cottages are fully self-contained, so all you need to bring is food and drinks – and your dog. Elm Cottage welcomes pets and there is no surcharge. Dog bowls, treats and poo bags are provided. There is even a Tesla charger available.

Northern Territory

A Good Rest B&B, Alice Springs

This is exclusive, executive-style, tourism-accredited bed and breakfast accommodation, with fully self-contained, air-conditioned private villas with their own private entrance, queen and king single beds. This is a great spot to explore the Red Centre and enjoy a town like Alice.

Alice on Todd Apartments, Alice Springs

Alice on Todd Apartments offers a choice of 57 fully self-contained studio, one-bedroom, one-bedroom deluxe, two-bedroom and two-bedroom deluxe apartments to suit all types of traveller. Alice on Todd Apartments provides a clean, comfortable and spacious option for visitors to Alice Springs.

Golden Sands Retreat Beach House, Darwin

Golden Sands Retreat is a beautiful absolute beachfront property. There are also cabins on the property. This is an ideally located spot for you to explore the surrounds of the northern capital. Take your dog for a visit to Mindil Beach Markets, take in a sunset drink at the famous Darwin Ski Club or visit the dog-friendly parks in the area.

The Beach Shack, Dundee Beach

This is a great getaway situated on the beachfront and close to the Lodge of Dundee. Whether you are looking for a quiet family getaway from the hustle and bustle of the city, or a week-long fishing trip with your mates, you will find spectacular views overlooking Fogg Bay. Sit back, relax and watch the beautiful Top End sunsets while enjoying a sundowner on the front verandah. This two-bedroom property sleeps seven people comfortably and is fully maintained.

Victoria River Retreat, Timber Creek

The Victoria River Retreat has three air-conditioned bedrooms with a queen, double and two single beds. There is a modern, fully equipped kitchen with plenty of space, leading out to a huge deck with a barbecue. There is plenty of space outside for boats and four-wheel drives, including a double carport and large lawn area. Located in a quiet part of town, the house is minutes away from the Victoria River and Gregory National Park. Timber Creek is located on the Victoria River, 220 kilometres east of Kununurra in Western Australia and 280 kilometres west of Katherine in the Northern Territory. This is about as remote as it gets for a pet-friendly holiday house.

Queensland

Floriana Villas, Cairns

Boutique, stylish Spanish-mission style apartments on The Esplanade in Cairns. Just a short walk to everything on offer.

Belmara Coolum Holiday Unit, Coolum

This comfortable three-bedroom unit is close to public transport, parks, shops, restaurants and a safe, patrolled beach. You'll love the place because of the location and the outdoor space for your dog to play in. The property is close to the beach and has ocean views.

Puppies and Pancakes, Coolum Beach

Fully equipped, two-bedroom unit, with ground-level private entry and a huge backyard for exclusive use of guests and their fellow furry travellers. Hear the ocean from the backyard, feel sea breezes, and beach access to an off-lead dog beach is just a kilometre away from the house. The property is not suitable for young children but is perfect for your fur baby.

Gum Tree Lodge and Bush Camp, Howard

Just off the highway at Howard this is another place with a lot of buzz on the online travel forums for dog owners who are on the road year-round. They have a lovely guest suite that is dog-friendly and the whole place is set on 40 acres so there is plenty of space for walking.

Mena Creek Falls Guest House, Mena Creek

Situated only 200 metres from the park is this recently restored and renovated church from the 1950s. The owners have painstakingly restored this amazing chapel to its former beauty and have tried to ensure you have everything that you would expect to have at a unique luxury stay with all the mod cons. Perfectly situated in the heart of Mena Creek you are a two-minute walk to Paronella Park, Mena Creek Falls, the pub and general store.

Serenity, Mudjimba (Sunshine Coast)

Mudjimba has a surprising number of holiday rentals that accept dogs. Serenity is an eco-friendly family beach house designed to make you feel relaxed and refreshed. The spacious home has high, exposed wooden ceilings and a range of chill-out areas to cater to all needs. The alfresco dining area overlooks the pool and is next to the massive open plan kitchen/lounge area.

Cabana@Cupania, Mudjimba (Sunshine Coast)

This newly renovated house is only two minutes' walk to the fully patrolled, dog-friendly Mudjimba Beach. It's also wheelchair-friendly, pet-friendly and has so many living areas (including a games room with full-size pool table – teenager-friendly!) that everyone can have their own kind of holiday. Set over two floors with polished floorboards, this three-bedroom, three-bathroom home immediately makes you feel relaxed.

The Island, Mudjimba (Sunshine Coast)

This home impresses on every level and it is located on Mudjimba Esplanade, opposite fully patrolled and dog-friendly Mudjimba Beach. Let your dog have a fantastic holiday, too. Upstairs consists of a very large lounge and dining area with high, vaulted ceilings with a fully integrated contemporary kitchen.

Scarness Cottage, Scarness

Two-bedroom cottage with a pool and lovely outdoor areas for you and your pooch. Just 350 metres to an off-lead beach, the house is also a short walk to the local pub and many restaurants on the Esplanade. It is also close to parkland for walks with the dog, and a short drive to all the facilities you will need.

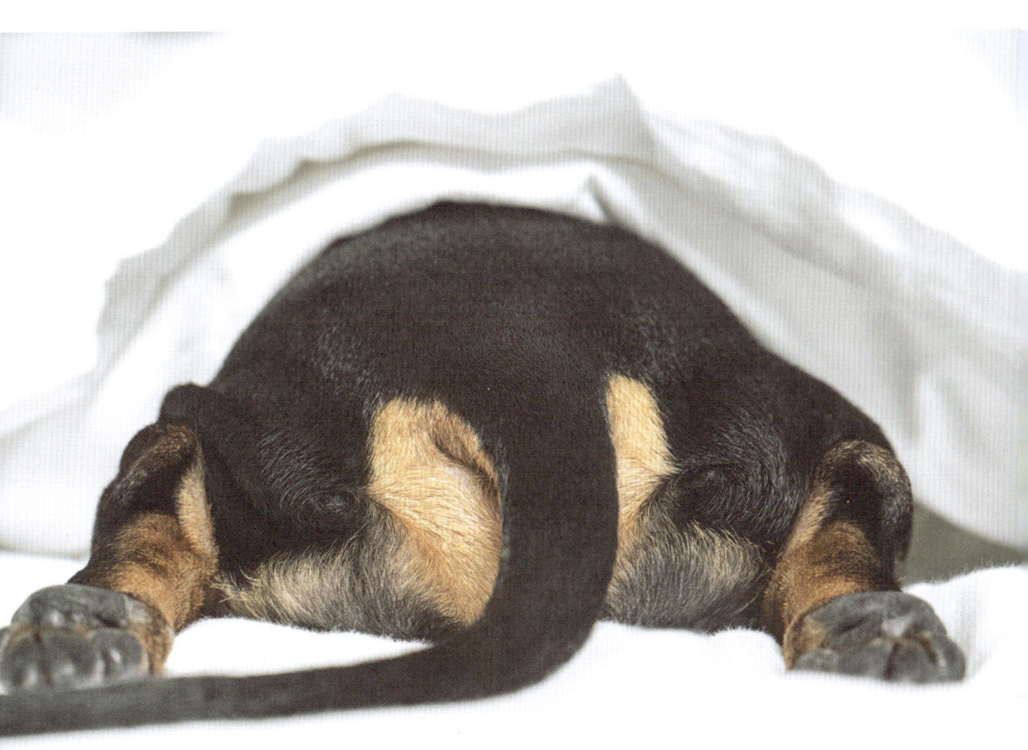

TRAVEL TAILS

Virginia and Raphael Chang and Pancho the Australian bulldog (@pancho_theaussiebulldog)

Pancho is a well-travelled pooch that has burned rubber from Port Douglas in Queensland to Mt Gambier in South Australia. Virginia Chang is pleased that things are changing when it comes to dog-friendliness and notes that it was only recently that Booking.com included a filter for pet-friendly stays.

'Before that it was really hard and you had to rely on blogs,' she says. 'Even now the term "dog-friendly" is really misused. There are many places that you go and you realise they are not really pet-friendly and they ask you to leave your pet outdoors.'

Chang has found that the New South Wales South Coast is a particularly dog-friendly spot but Cairns is not, due to the high concentration of national parks and no-go areas. She spends a lot of time at Eden and Merimbula and is also a fan of Lakes Entrance in Gippsland, Victoria. But she recommends checking the seasons as during peak times there are more restrictions on where dogs can go, particularly on the local beaches.

Chang does not camp with Pancho, preferring her accommodation to come with four solid walls and a roof. She mainly uses Airbnb and suggests putting on the pet-friendly filter but warns that you have to make sure what they mean when they say pets are welcome.

'I will always contact them now as we made the mistake once of thinking a place was pet-friendly and then he was not allowed inside. Now we stay at the Goat & Goose on Airbnb at Lakes Entrance,' she says. 'They are really good because they have a private balcony where you can have your pet inside or outside.' In Eden they stay in the Eden Motel.

Another thing Chang says that you need to check when renting a holiday home is if there are any restrictions on the weight of your dog. 'I guess they do it to gauge the size of your dog,' she says. 'But Pancho, being a bulldog, he is chubby by nature and using weight is not reliable. How is the weight relevant? So I call in advance to avoid any disappointment.'

When they did go to Cairns, Chang made sure that although Pancho was not able to travel to the Great Barrier Reef with them that he had a good holiday of his own while they were away.

'We planned in advance to make sure he also had a good time,' Chang says. 'We booked him a daycare place where he could stay and he even had a hydrobath. He actually had a holiday of his own.'

South Australia

Thirty-Two JW, Ardrossan

Located amongst a small group of traditional shacks, Thirty-Two JW is a cute, cosy and comfortable three-bedroom beachfront property located in the peaceful holiday destination of James Well on beautiful York Peninsula. The shack has a warm, inviting atmosphere and comprises three bedrooms, sleeping six (one queen bed, one double bed and one set of bunk beds).

Jack's House, Clare

This gorgeous old three-bedroom house with a cottage garden surrounded by a picket fence is located in the heart of Clare. It has been beautifully updated with all the mod-cons, there is a fully equipped kitchen and your breakfast provisions are included. The popular Riesling Trail cycling route through the wine country runs nearby, and you are just a short walk to the centre of Clare and close to all the Clare Valley restaurants and wineries. Perfect for the whole family: big, small or furry!

Vandy's Shack at Dutton Bay, Lower Eyre Peninsula

Vandy's Shack is on the absolute beachfront with comfortable retro decor and has two bedrooms, sleeping five. Make the most of the waterfront location with the kayaks available to use during your stay. And don't forget to get down and sample some famous Coffin Bay oysters straight from the calm waters of the bay.

The Shack, Goolwa North

A lovely, newly refurbished one-bedroom shack, this is the perfect place for a couple wanting a relaxing weekend away. Stroll down to the town's cafe, shops, restaurants and the mighty Murray River or simply relax at home with a barbecue. This shack caters for humans and their pets, offering a large fully enclosed yard with ample parking space for cars and boats.

Hideaway Tom's on Mundoo Channel, Hindmarsh Island

Absolute waterfront, freshly renovated, modern and stylish two-bedroom house on Mundoo Channel, Hindmarsh Island. Located within the waters of the Coorong National Park with a private jetty and fully enclosed yard. A tranquil, peaceful setting with abundant birdlife to watch from a fabulous, protected outdoor patio area. The house also has an outdoor fire pit for the cooler months.

The Eyrie, Marion Bay

Enjoy the beautiful coastal lifestyle of Marion Bay and Innes National Park. There is something here for everyone: surfing, fishing, native birds and wildlife, beautiful beaches and spectacular coastline to explore. The house is right on the boundary of the national park, and only a five-minute walk from Willyama Beach. Backing onto a reserve, there are sweeping views of native scrub and salt lakes, and the reserve is a great place for heading off for walks with your pawed pal. Note that the yard is not fenced so you will need to keep your pup on the covered balcony. You'll also need to bring your own bed linen and towels.

Crystal Blue Apartment, Port Vincent

Crystal Blue is a modern, first floor, beachside holiday apartment located in the centre of Port Vincent, overlooking the crystal blue waters of St Vincent Gulf. Crystal Blue is fully self-contained and can accommodate up to six people, although it is best suited for a couple – and their doggo.

Marley's at Robe, Robe

Just 50 metres from beautiful Long Beach, this modern, spacious beach house has a huge open-plan living area drenched with natural light, designed especially with holidaymakers in mind. There is plenty of space with a designer kitchen, two living spaces and a large grassy garden for your pup. Luxuriously finished with quality furnishings and styling, the master bedroom has a king bed, flat screen TV, walk in robe and ensuite.

Sea Retro Getaway, Semaphore

This unique beach house with original 1960s architecture and decor is located just five houses from Semaphore Beach and less than four minutes walk to Semaphore Road, which boasts more than 15 restaurants, cafes, supermarkets, a major cinema, and more. Across the Port River is Port Adelaide with many historical sites, river cruises, art galleries and dolphin watching from canoes.

Perlubie Sea Luxury Villas, Eyre Peninsula

Perlubie Landing is a spectacular hidden gem. There are two architecturally designed eco-friendly villas, Black and White, and each villa has a king-sized bed, lounge area, air conditioning, bath, shower, kitchenette, and a deck with a barbecue and outdoor seating. Every room has a view overlooking the Southern Ocean. Note that while pets are welcome, the yard is not fenced.

Melaleuca, Venus Bay, Eyre Peninsula

Melaleuca cabin has access to Harbor Point's private beach, set on 70 acres of virgin native vegetation, wonderful for nature walks along the cliff tops and bird watching. Its own private beachfront allows small boats and canoes to be launched and moored for easy access to your favourite whiting spot or to explore an island. The cabin is eco friendly, utilising solar power and rainwater, and maximises the scenic views of the bay spanning from Venus Bay past the islands to Port Kenny, with wonderful sunsets and the lights of the two towns by night. Plus, it has a lockable dog kennel for your pet's holiday safety.

Tasmania

Arthur River Spa Cottage, Arthur River

This amazing waterfront beach house located on the north-west tip of Tasmania has an open fire in the lounge room and a huge two-person spa bath in the king-sized bedroom, as well as satellite TV and three large bedrooms. The place sleeps 10 including the double sofa bed in the lounge. There is direct access to the mirror-calm Arthur River, flanked by Australia's largest temperate rain forest.

Self Contained Holiday Unit, Bicheno

Located a short walk from the beach, this cosy two-bedroom cottage can sleep up to six. There is a very pleasant manicured garden with a barbecue area, and if you need a bit of solitude or a quiet glass of wine, the gazebo will be just perfect.

Pelicans Rest, Boomer Bay

This is a great spot to unwind in a fully self-contained holiday house. The large decks make outdoor living, and hanging out with your dog, easy, with plenty of room for a barbecue as well. The holiday home is just 35 minutes from Hobart airport and a halfway stop between Hobart and Port Arthur – you can visit the Port Arthur Historic Site, which is famously dog-friendly (see page 161 for details).

Roaring Beach Retreat, Bruny Island

Looking for the perfect getaway relaxing by the beach? Roaring Beach Retreat has stunning views overlooking the white sandy beach, as well as the natural country charm of green rolling hills to the back. Wake up to these magnificent views and fall asleep to the sound of the waves rolling in. Roaring Beach Retreat is situated a short 10-minute drive from the town of Dover where all supplies can be found as well as restaurants.

A Place to Stay in Derby, Derby

Fully renovated miner's cottage 750 metres from the head of the Blue Derby mountain biking trail network, which is also a great place to walk your dog. There is a light and spacious lounge and dining area and a heat pump and wood fire for the colder weather. The place accommodates six in comfortable beds with hotel-grade linen.

Castaway Cottage, Dover

Charming on the outside and beautifully appointed and modern on the inside, with your own private garden and barbecue area, and just a grassy reserve between you and the beach. Castaway Cottage makes the ideal destination for a romantic retreat or a family beachside holiday. There are two stunning bedrooms with gorgeous views over Port Esperance Bay, a brand-new bathroom with a luxurious bath for two and a kitchen to impress even the most hardcore chef.

Peck's on Pine, Hobart

Why not have your very own Victorian Cottage for the price of a hotel room? This Victorian weatherboard was built in 1891 and is a fully self-contained, pet-friendly bed and breakfast cottage. The place features stained-glass windows and is furnished with antique pieces and collectables. This cosy accommodation offers a living and dining room, double bedroom, separate bathroom and a private courtyard. The cottage is ideally suited for a couple and their pooch. The fully stocked kitchen is equipped with all the modern conveniences so it is just like a home away from home for you and your pet.

Pam's Place, Huon Valley

Pam's Place is a two-bedroom, self-contained house in scenic Eggs and Bacon Bay, near Cygnet, Tasmania. The two bedrooms have queen beds and all kitchen utensils, crockery, cutlery and linen are supplied, as are laundry facilities. Pam's Place has undercover car parking for two vehicles. The yard is fully fenced and is totally proofed against any canine escape artists. You are just a three-minute walk to the protected beach and an hour's drive from Hobart and the Salamanca Markets. Explore the Huon Valley, visit a local winery, cidery or gallery or just go bush walking, kayaking or swimming with your family and best friend.

Penfold Cottage, Launceston

This property is centrally located to everything Launceston has to offer. The spacious three-bedroom home features polished floorboards, a brand-new kitchen and bathroom, reverse-cycle air conditioning, sunroom and a large, fenced yard.

Halcyon Days, St Helens

The cosy dwelling has a large deck at the rear with views down to the bay filtered by beautiful big gum trees. It is a very relaxing spot to take in the surrounding serenity. The house has two bedrooms accommodating four guests and an open-plan dining, lounge and kitchen area. Off-street parking is available and Halcyon Days has a large, fenced yard that can accommodate well-behaved dogs that don't want to miss out on the family holiday.

Victoria

Pickett Cottage, Beechworth

Pickett Cottage is the perfect choice for a couple and their fur baby looking for a luxury, quiet, holiday break. The cosy cottage is packed with period features and has a fenced garden. It is located right in the heart of town only 50 metres to specialty shops, cafes and Beechworth's finest restaurants.

St Peter's Accommodation, Cape Bridgewater

Only a short drive from the pristine Bridgewater Bay, Discovery Bay and 20 minutes from Portland is the magnificently restored St Peter's Church, which was built in 1883. This represents a very different stay for you and your pet and is an online favourite.

Rickie's Shack, Echuca

Rickie's Shack is actually a spacious, older-style two-bedroom home in Echuca within walking distance to the historic port area and town centre as well as the Murray Riverwalk. It's in a quiet street with an outside entertaining area for your dog to roam in.

Murray River Houseboats, Echuca

A different sort of house, of the floating kind, but there are some dog-friendly boats available for cruising the Murray River. This is a great old-school way to travel and is perfect for dogs that can handle the river life. Pull up at a pub or park and just jump off – it can put some of the spontaneity back into doggy travels.

The Grove, Gunbower

The Grove is a spacious three-bedroom farmhouse with a secure dog yard. If you love peace, tranquillity and wildlife then this is the place for you. There is a ton of bird life when you are walking your dog along the banks of the Gunny Creek and you and Rover might even spot a wallaby or two.

Janaza Boutique Retreat, Halls Gap

See the spectacular scenery of the Grampians in a luxurious, architecturally designed holiday retreat. This stunning, spacious one-bedroom boutique accommodation has contemporary furnishings and the secluded panoramic mountain views make for an unforgettable experience.

Goat & Goose B&B, Lakes Entrance

This traditional B&B (you will be sharing the accommodation with other guests) has stunning ocean views and a private balcony so you can have your dog inside or out. Continental breakfast is included or you can pay extra for a full cooked breakfast.

White Willow Escape, Macs Cove

Bring the boat, bring the fishing rods, visit the snow or come and explore the best of what the High Country has to offer no matter the season. Set in the quaint and peaceful township of Macs Cove and only a stone's throw from Lake Eildon. Get an alpine getaway for you and your pets.

Figtree Cottage, Mystery Bay

Set on a rural property between Narooma and Bermagui, it's just a short walk or drive to Mystery Bay beach for swimming, snorkelling or diving and walking with your canine friend. The cottage has a lovely secure garden.

Hollyoak, Trentham

A beautifully appointed English country-style home positioned just 300 metres from the Trentham Village centre. This place comes highly recommended by dog owners who sings its praises online.

Western Australia

Emu Point Beach Cottage (Oyster Cottage), Albany

Oyster Cottage is your home-away-from-home-by-the-sea, a fully equipped two-bedroom pet-friendly holiday unit. It is located on a quiet street overlooking a park, just 200 metres from gorgeous beaches, and 500 metres from the popular Emu Point Cafe and kids' play park.

Oyster Cottage has a dog trampoline bed and feed/water bowls. The large backyard is fenced on three sides but is not secured from the road because it shares a common driveway with Cockleshell cottage next door. There are many off-lead dog exercise areas around Emu Point.

The Retro Shack, Augusta

A cosy older-style beachside shack ideally located less than 50 metres from the water's edge. This piece of coastline has it all: swimming, fishing, surfing, kayaking and, of course, dog-walking. The refurbished Colourpatch Bar & Cafe (thecolourpatchaugusta.com) and mini golf are a five-minute stroll away. It is a beautiful 15-minute walk into town with a coffee stop along the way, and a 10-minute stroll to the historical settlement of Old Flinders where the protected waters of Granny's Pool are ideal for young children.

Driftwood Cottage, Busselton

At Driftwood Cottage you can come and enjoy the relaxing pace of the beautiful coastal town of Busselton with its famous jetty (which is sadly not dog-friendly). Quiet, secluded and surrounded by shady peppermint trees, Driftwood Cottage is a family-owned holiday house right in town. An easy 250-metre stroll brings you to the safe white beaches of Geographe Bay or to the main shopping precinct. There is a large kennel outside, a dog bed and a fully enclosed yard to keep Fido safe and happy.

Coastal Court, Denham

Coastal Court offers affordable accommodation in the heart of the Shark Bay Marine Park. The property is just a few minutes' walk from the beach, boat ramp and fishing jetty, playground, local supermarket, fuel station and restaurants. You will need to bring your own bed linen and towels. The house is not just pet-friendly but has a secure courtyard at the rear of the unit for your pet's safety.

Urchin Beach Cottage, Esperance

Urchin Cottage is just a 300-metre stroll to Castletown Beach. It is 200 metres from the main beach walk/bike tracks that take you to all playgrounds and to the beaches close to the town, so there is plenty of natural beauty for you and your pet to explore. The cottage has three large bedrooms and an enclosed grassy yard.

While dogs are permitted, the owner prefers them outside at all times in summer, but they can sleep inside in winter by prior arrangement and if they use their own bed. No dogs in bedrooms, on beds or on lounges.

30 Kennedy Street, Exmouth

This great three-bedroom, two-bathroom home is perfect for groups or families. Take a 500-metre leisurely stroll to the eateries, shops, and Exmouth town centre, or relax in front of the television after a big day on the water with your pooch.

Paddy's Golden Patch, Kalgoorlie

Budget two-bedroom apartment in Victory Heights, Kalgoorlie/Boulder a great base to explore the Goldfields area. There is a secure courtyard for your four-legged friend.

Karri Tree Cottage, Quinninup

Pet-friendly Karri Tree Cottage is located in peaceful Quinninup, just 20 minutes from Manjimup and Pemberton and one hour from Walpole. This comfy family home is located beside a stunning old growth native forest and adjacent to beautiful Karri Lake. The cottage is a large open-plan, two-bedroom home with a lounge containing a solid fuel wood heater, a well-appointed kitchen plus dining area, separate laundry and bathroom. Karri Tree Cottage has a unique and rustic charm and is sure to please those who appreciate a laidback country life. Relax on the verandah by day and in front of the log fire by night, perfect for families and friends or a romantic hideaway retreat, but pooch-friendly too.

Swan Valley Heights, Swan Valley

Swan Valley Heights sits up on the Scarp with unlimited views over the entire city of Perth. There are plenty of kangaroos to watch all day long as well as sheep grazing the property in case you have a dog that wants to exercise its shepherding instincts (from behind a safe fence, that is). This spacious home has a big open-plan lounge/dining area, a pool and lovely native gardens.

TRAVEL TAILS

Shandos Cleaver and Schnitzel the miniature dachshund

To say that Shandos Cleaver knows a thing or two about travelling with dogs is definitely an understatement. She is something of a pet-travel expert having taken her miniature dachshund Schnitzel not just all over Australia but all around the world. Cleaver records her adventures, as well as a range of her travel advice on her website and blog Travelnuity (travelnuity.com).

'My dog must be one of the most well-travelled dogs in the world,' Cleaver says. 'He's visited 35 countries, as well as travels around Australia [to NSW, Victoria and South Australia], we also travelled around Europe with him for over one and a half years, and he's also visited the United States.'

That is an impressive number of stamps in his pet passport but Schnitzel is part of Cleaver's family, so just like you wouldn't leave behind your human children, Cleaver does not like to leave him behind if she can help it.

'Flying a dog overseas from Australia is difficult, and it's even harder to return, but for our long trip to Europe and the United States it was worth the effort and cost to bring him along,' she says. 'When travelling in Australia, as long as you're not mainly visiting national parks, it's still possible to visit and do so much with a dog.'

As for travel tips, one of the most important for Cleaver is to make sure you know where you are going and what you are doing to be sure that the trip is suitable for your four-legged friend.

'Carefully consider the type of trip that you're taking and the regulations that apply before committing to travelling with a dog,' she says. 'While I've travelled overseas with my dog, I wouldn't recommend it for short trips or to certain destinations.

Training your dog in advance, including crate training, is also advantageous.'

Cleaver has just taken off to complete the 'Big Lap' around Australia with Schnitzel so he is set to clock up even more frequent doggy traveller miles.

CHAPTER SEVEN

THINGS TO DO

Here comes Sandy Claws: where can you take your dog to the beach?

Australia's beaches are one of the great places to take your dog for a walk. But, like planes and cafes, we do lag behind the rest of the world in our dog friendliness.

Dogs are not allowed on all beaches, and not at all if they are inside a national park (with a few exceptions). In Sydney, for example, dogs are allowed at just a handful of coastal locations despite the huge number of beaches, and dog owners, in the New South Wales capital.

A fair number of beaches in Australia are shared beaches meaning that dogs have a curfew that might be a time of day or a time of year that they are allowed to frolic on the foreshore (they have more freedom to roam in winter, generally, with summer the domain of humans). There is usually clear signage to this effect.

There are few places where a poo bag is more essential. There is nothing so obvious as a dog poo sitting on pristine sand, and you cannot bury it without the risk of seriously ruining someone's future day out making sandcastles. If you are fortunate enough to find a lead-free beach then make sure your dog is under effective control because it's pretty embarrassing if your dog kicks sand in someone's face while they are having a quiet picnic, or shakes themselves all over a stranger's dry towel.

Dog safety on the sand

The first thing to remember is that, despite having a swimming stroke named after them (dog paddle), not all dogs are good swimmers, and no dogs are natural swimmers; they all need to learn what to do in the water. Some dogs may be anxious in the water, some breeds, like dachshunds, simply lack the leg length to be canine Ian Thorpes. While other breeds, like the setter and retriever, were bred for the water and may be as elegant in the sea as a team of synchronised swimmers.

As an owner of a water-loving Old English sheepdog, our dog was fine as a puppy, or when he is clipped, but as an adult his full coat can be heavy enough to drag him down and drown him. Make sure you stay within your dog's, and your, capabilities while you are at the beach. For all breeds you might want to think about a floatation device (see page 22 of the gear section) if you are unsure how they will go the first time in the sea.

Rinse your dog off after its swim because breeds that are prone to skin irritations can find the salt makes their skin itch.

Keep a close eye on your dog too. A lot of strange things wash up on beaches, from medical waste to bluebottles with a fairly unpleasant sting. If you are walking in rock pools remember that the blue-ringed octopus can be as deadly to dogs as they can be to humans. If you are rock pool hopping also be sure to check the tides or you may end up stranded with a pooch who does not swim as well as you do.

Bring fresh water, because dogs new to the ocean will try to drink the seawater and that can make them unwell and make for a very messy car ride back home.

Dogs can get sunburnt. Make sure they are not out in the sun too long or consider applying some protection like Petkin Doggy Sunstick (petcircle.com.au).

Finally, if the sand it too hot for your feet then it is too hot for your dog's paws. Their pads can burn and blister and you risk infection in such a difficult area to isolate for recovery.

Below is a selection of our favourite dog-friendly beaches for each state and some of the rules.

Australian Capital Territory

Not to be left out, despite the fact it is a land-locked state, Canberra allows a host of places where dogs can go for a dip in its famous lakes. There are even a bunch of new dog swimming areas that can be found in south, central and north Canberra, including: Lake Tuggeranong, Greenway; Orana Bay, Yarralumla; Kurrajong Point beach, Weston Park, Yarralumla; Yerrabi Pond, Gungahlin; several locations at Lake Ginninderra in Belconnen, including Diddams Close.

New South Wales

Denhams Beach, Batemans Bay

This rocky beach is protected from the elements and at low tide you can wander around as far as Wimbie Beach. It is not all off-lead though so be sure to check the signs.

Callala Beach, Jervis Bay

This relatively undiscovered part of the popular bay is off-lead from 4 pm to 8 am and on-lead at other times. Enter through one of the overgrown walking paths to pristine sand and waves with dolphins catching a ride. Nearby Hyams Beach (about 30 minutes' drive south) is more popular and lays claim to the whitest sand in the country – and you can walk on-lead there.

Moonee Beach, Coffs Harbour

This is an on-lead beach but has great variety, from swimming in the surf to a picturesque walk out to the headland. Moonee Beach Market Place even has a place for a puppuccino in Maggie's Dog Cafe that was voted Australia's most dog-friendly cafe in 2020 (maggiesdogcafe.com) – it also has a dog spa and retail outlet.

Sirius Cove, Sydney

Virtually the only off-lead patch of sand on the northern harbourside (timeshare on weekends), this small Mosman beach is protected by a rock wall and the water is calm and shallow enough that you can swim with your dog just metres from the moored yachts of Mosman locals. A great place to introduce your dog to the water.

Kurnell Beach, Sydney

This southern city beach was the landing spot of James Cook and has a large off-lead area between the third and fourth rock groynes at the western end of Silver Beach. It is a great spot for whale watching in season too.

Northern Territory

Casuarina Coastal Reserve, Darwin

The NT has a similar view to Western Australia when it comes to 'effective control'. If you have a dog that will respond immediately to voice recall then you have a bit more freedom than if you have a more strong-willed dog. Dogs are welcome to be off-lead in this coastal hotspot between Rapid Creek and Sandy Creek if they are well behaved.

Queensland

Red Beach, Bribie Island

Island paradise awaits you and your best friend and it is just a short walk away (over a convenient bridge) where you can share a Moreton Bay sunset together and go for a run on the sand.

Ellis Beach, Cairns

We know it can get a bit a loose up north, and Cairns offers a huge array of on- and off-lead options for dog owners, far more choice than in the southern state. The rocky shore of Ellis Beach is one of the most interesting though and well worth a look.

The Gold Coast

For an area famed for its beaches it is good to know that dogs have a few options on the Goldie. Best known is probably The Spit where you have a huge stretch of sand and dunes to do the zoomies on. But you can also visit Tallebudgera, Currumbin and Biggera Waters Beach.

Warrana Beach, Sunshine Coast

Nine kilometres of unspoilt sand and just a plastic spade's throw from some of the great beachside cafes of this part of the coast.

Pallarenda Beach, Townsville

This is a huge stretch of coast that looks onto the magnificent boulders of Magnetic Island, so precariously balanced that early settlers thought they must be magnetised. Dogs cannot have the whole beach, but there are designated zones that they can cut loose in.

Tasmania

Cosy Corner, Bay of Fires

There are a few stretches of this incredible coastline that allow on-lead beach action as well as camping in amongst the red-hued rocks. Break O'Day Council has a list of detailed restrictions and dogs are banned from Jeanneret Beach.

Bicheno

This stretch of coast on Tasmania's east coast is lead-free around the river mouth and the southern end of Denison Beach, with on-lead access to other parts of the coast. Grab some calamari or flathead fillets straight off the boat from The Gulch, a fish and chips and fresh seafood shack at the end of a jetty.

Adams Beach, Bridport

The wide sand flats of this beach are off-lead year-round and so quiet you might even land the whole beach to yourself.

South Australia

Glenelg Beach, Adelaide

South Australia is pretty good with dog access to beaches with most beaches in the city allowing on-lead walks between 10 am and 8 pm. Our pick of the bunch is Glenelg Beach but West Beach is also a good option.

Kangaroo Island

Though there are no dedicated off-lead areas on this island you are permitted to have your dog off-lead if it is 'under effective voice command', so well-trained pups can wander the beaches there.

O'Sullivan Beach, Onkaparinga

This protected bay on the Fleurieu Peninsula is popular for fishing and boating and offers off-lead access for dogs year-round.

TRAVEL TAILS

Eva Kobes, Kiran Patel and Maisie (@maisie_the_border_collie)

At just over a year and half old, Maisie the border collie, has travelled places and done things that many humans would envy.

On a trip from Perth to Exmouth, the person-loving pooch was treated just like any other member of the family and was never left behind; whether it was sunsets on the beach, swimming in the surf or an ocean cruise to see the dolphins of Monkey Mia.

The three travellers took a Perfect Nature cruise at Monkey Mia that was an amazing experience. 'Maisie had never been on a boat in her life,' says Kobes. 'But she was really good, she was scared at first with the sound of the motor and the sail popping up but after a while she was fine. It was a three-hour cruise and we saw eagle rays, dolphins, turtles, dugongs, we were really lucky. And Maisie saw all that, too.'

Kobes recommends enjoying Monkey Mia sunsets with your pooch in the sheltered bay where the waves are calm for dogs that are not great swimmers. Dogs are allowed on certain parts of the beach but, like humans, must get out of the water if a pod of dolphins arrives.

'One sunset we had turtles in the bay and the second night we had eight dolphins just swimming around while we were watching the sunset, which was pretty special,' Kobes says.

The travellers found Coral Bay a bit more limiting due to the huge marine park. There is a caravan park that takes pets but there is not a lot of things you can do. But there was the best beach that the trio had ever been to, so it was worth the trip.

'Five Fingers Beach was our favourite beach,' she says. 'It is called Five Fingers because when you look on Google Maps on the satellite image you can see the fingers of reef extending to the beach. I couldn't believe this beach was dog-friendly to be honest because it was such an amazing spot to go snorkelling.'

On the trip the trio spent a lot of time off-road as they love to four-wheel drive and they stayed at Bruboodjoo Campground, Wooramel River Retreat and the RAC Resort in Monkey Mia. All in all, the trip was a huge success and they also recently took a drive down south to Albany.

'We did make sure we got a lot of national parks out of our system,' Kobes laughs. 'But our dog is like our kid – we don't have any kids so far, so it is important to take her with us as much as we can. She's our pet, she's our baby and we want to do adventures together.'

Victoria

Ninety Mile Beach, Gippsland

As its name suggests, there is so much sand to go round here that you might find you have the entire beach, and its wild windswept beauty, all to yourself – and your pup. Cape Conran is one of the rare national park beaches that allow dogs on-lead, and you can stay in the campground just metres from the sand where each campsite comes with its own fire pit. One of the best beach camps for dog lovers in the state.

The Great Ocean Road

Victoria's most famous coastal drive has a range of dog-friendly options with Torquay, Anglesea and Lorne all having year-round off-lead options for travellers. Point Addis, a stunning beach surrounded by crumbling cliffs, allows dogs on-lead.

Brighton Beach, Melbourne

This off-lead dog beach has shallow waves for the littlies, plenty of sand for big-dog running, and then you can head to Sandy Beach HQ, a cafe in the charming old boat shed with black-and-white historic photos of this beachy suburb adorning the walls; sandybeachhq.com.au

Safety Beach, Mornington Peninsula

Another cliff-bound patch of sand with plenty of rockpools to explore as well, plus you can also take your dog to the nearby town of Dromana.

YCW Beach, Phillip Island

This island break is a great spot for families and pets, but due to the colonies of penguins your pooch will have to be on a lead at all times. That said this surf beach is a great place for a walk and to admire the island beauty.

Western Australia

Cable Beach, Broome

This famous stretch of sand, best known for the much-photographed camel rides that take place at sunset, is also a great spot to spend sundown with your faithful companion.

South Beach, Fremantle

For beginner doggy paddlers, this beach has waves that lap gently and a huge grassy area to burn off some excess energy.

Margaret River

The White Elephant Cafe in Gnarabup (whiteelephantcafe.com.au) might just be the best beach spot you will ever take your dog – and it has great food and coffee to boot. This cafe is right on the dog-friendly beach in Margaret River. You can also take dogs for a lead-free visit to Geographe Bay, Bunker Bay and Yallingup Beach.

South City Beach, Perth

Perth residents are a bit spoiled for choice for dog beaches. There are a number of the west-coast beaches that are off-lead too, such as South City Beach. This is a well-to-do part of Perth with beachside cafes and has often taken the title of best city beach.

Barks and recreation: the best pet-friendly activities (that are not just dog parks)

It is all very well to hit the road with your pet but, like it or not, travelling with your dog does limit what you can do. As we have touched upon, Australia does not lead the world in dog-friendliness despite a wealth of dog owners, and a recent surge in new doggy parents as a result of the state lockdowns and COVID-19. Yes, you can take your dog for a walk most places on a lead – and finding a dog park is the first order of business when you land for the night – but what about more interesting activities for you and your travelling fido to indulge in?

Charlie Brincat started his business Herding Dog Training Melbourne ('herding training for city dogs'; herdingdogtraining.com) 10 years ago when he thought he was buying a Labrador but ended up with a kelpie, a dog that would lead him to his new business in Melbourne's outer suburbs.

'We took it to puppy school and the trainer basically kicked us out of school and said that our dog was disrupting the class because, as a kelpie, he just wanted to run; he was not the sort of dog to sit by your side. He said, "Your dog really needs to go and chase some sheep," so I found someone in Gippsland that trained farm dogs and once I saw the instinct in our kelpie I was hooked.'

Brincat continued to train his dog for years and, when he gained enough knowledge himself, he thought there were other city folk, like him, who might want to learn more about their working dogs. He leased some land and bought some sheep a little bit closer to the city and invited people to bring their city dogs up and see what sort of a herder they are.

'They must have the instinct,' he says. 'We have a group session, introduce them to the sheep and see what their dog can do. The kelpies and the collies are the two working dogs we use mostly in Australia and their instinct is to go to the stock and bring it to you. But the amount of that instinct left after years of breeding without working, the instinct is different in each dog, the best ones are still the ones that are bred on farms.'

The people that attend the classes tend to be people who say their dog has no recall in the park, or it is rounding up their kids. Many people only come once to see what the dog is capable of but others come regularly to continue the training. Puppies are welcome and one of the joys for Brincat is to watch even the youngest of dogs start working.

'City people are generally very loving with their dogs,' Brincat says, 'but a lot of people have the wrong idea of what these dogs need, so understanding them better can help with that.'

As pet owners we know that most of the attractions that pets are allowed in are mostly outdoor ones – parks and trails, rivers and lakes. That said we have rounded up a few of the more urban and unusual places that you can go with your four-legged friend around Australia.

Australian Capital Territory

The National Arboretum

This national treasure in the heart of Canberra offers over 44,000 rare and endangered trees for your dog to cock its leg on. There are a wealth of interesting trails across a 250-hectare site, as well as great cafe inside the modern, high-ceilinged information centre. And walk to the top of the property with your pooch for one of the best views of the national capital.

nationalarboretum.act.gov.au

Go Boating on Lake Burley Griffin

Hire a pedal boat on the shores of Canberra's famous lake and you can take your dog with you. The boats seat two adults with room for a pooch in between and you can pedal at a nice slow pace around the lake between the two bridges at Regatta Point.

capitalpaddle.com.au

Central Loop Walk

Known as the bridge-to-bridge walk by locals, this walk heads in a circle between Commonwealth Avenue Bridge and Kings Avenue Bridge and cuts in near the National Gallery of Australia. These days you have to keep your eye out for some of the zippier road users who are taking advantage of the new electric scooters, but they are speed limited, so just keep an eye on your pup.

Parliament House

Yes, it is your dog's parliament too, so pooches are allowed access on to the lawns surrounding our cradle of democracy. You can then stroll the whole Parliament area taking in sights like Old Parliament House and the National Library (from the outside, sadly, with pets).
aph.gov.au

Mount Ainslie

This bird's eye view of the national capital allows you to fully appreciate Walter Burley Griffin's design. You don't have to walk all the way either, you can drive most of the way up to the car park, but for the hearty who wish to attempt the walk from the bottom you can take dogs through the Mount Ainslie Nature Reserve as long as they are on a lead.
visitcanberra.com.au

National Gallery of Australia Sculpture Garden

Wrapping around the gallery, this permanent outdoor sculpture exhibition allows you and your dog to soak up a bit of culture. The heavily designed garden showcases 26 sculptures made by international and Australian artists. Most of the sculptures were bought and placed in the garden during the early 1980s and they 'reflect the abstract, industrial aesthetic of that time' according to the NGA. But it is a great walk and a rare mixing of art and doggies.
nga.gov.au/sculpturegarden

The Kingston Foreshore

The hip suburb is a great place to walk your dog in Canberra with most restaurants facing the water and a great foreshore track to tire out your dog on. When they have barked at enough black swans, you can take a break at the Beef & Barley that is famous for its burger high tea and a yuzu martini.
beefandbarley.com.au

Murrumbateman Winery

When you are in this highly regarded wine region it seems churlish to leave without sampling some of the local drops and there are few more dog-friendly options than the Murrumbateman Winery. Not only does the winery welcome dogs but their very own winery dog, Mollie, hosts a range of special events year-round. Howlin' in the Vines is a pup-forward party at the cellar door so keep an eye on their Facebook page for upcoming events.

facebook.com/murrumbatemanwinery

New South Wales

Do Some 'Doga', Mosman

Where else but Sydney's pampered pooch capital would you find a yoga class dedicated to dogs? Rancan Sisters Fitness offers dog yoga classes that have found fame on TV and are held outdoors and require no yoga experience. Smaller dogs are incorporated into some of the doga positions while larger breeds will have to do their own contortions.
rancansistersfitness.com.au

Cool Off in the Pool, Alexandria

Sydney's first dog-friendly pool opened recently near the pooch-perfect grounds of Sydney Park. Located at the southern end of the park the dog-only pool allows pets to cool off in the middle of a long walk and is an initiative by dog-loving Sydney Lord Mayor Clover Moore.
cityofsydney.nsw.gov.au/parks/sydney-park

Centennial Parklands

This is more than just a dog-friendly park. Known as the 'green lungs' of Sydney in much the same way as Central Park is to New York, this sprawling parkland in the centre of the city takes in Moore Park, Centennial Park and Queens Park and more than a third is designated off-lead. A map is available on the website that shows where dogs are allowed both on- and off-lead.
centennialparklands.com.au/dogs

Moonlight Cinema

In Sydney's warmer months, Moonlight Cinema is a great evening out for you and your furry friend, with new release films showing on a huge inflatable screen in Centennial Park. You can also take your dog to Moonlight Cinemas in Adelaide, Brisbane, Melbourne and Perth.
moonlight.com.au

Sydney's Dog-Friendliest Pub

Woolloomooloo's Old Fitzroy is the rarest of beasts that allows your dog inside the pub to curl up under the pub table while you dine on innovative pub meals. Plus, there are loads of craft beers on tap to choose from. Just don't sit at the 'local's table' or disturb the wiry old Irish wolfhound asleep underneath.

oldfitzroy.com.au

Carriageworks Weekly Market

The farmers' market at Carriageworks, the redeveloped old train sheds near Redfern station, offers some of Sydney's best produce that you can buy and browse with lead in hand. Each Saturday morning the market attracts scores of dogs who bring their humans along to help them shop, including gourmet food and treats for pampered pooches. The nearby gallery may be less pup-friendly but drop in and have a look while your dog watches the world go by.

carriageworks.com.au

Get a Makeover at Hachi

This is more than just a groomer; things get a bit Sydney with a dog spa and photo studio in inner-city Haymarket. Hachi also has a dog cafe, regular events and a range of stylish dog clothes and accessories.
hachi-sydney.com.au

Go Whale Watching

The south coast has some of the best land-based whale-watching opportunities on the east coast. Head to the clifftops of Beecroft Peninsula, visit Point Perpendicular Lighthouse or the coast along Mollymook. Bonus: Bannisters has pet-friendly rooms for guests who want to visit Rick Stein's restaurant.
bannisters.com.au

See the Dog on the Tuckerbox, Gundagai

This is a must-stop spot for road trippers from Sydney to Melbourne so you may as well take your furry family member to meet the legendary dog statue. If you are not in a hurry you can also call in to the town of Temora and see another canine immortalised in metal. Boofhead the railway dog turned up one day in the country town after riding the rails all alone and was adopted by the station.

Hill End Historic Site, Mudgee

The remains of a once-thriving gold-mining community are now a living outdoor museum near the organics vineyards of Mudgee. The 8000 residents may have moved on but wandering the rusted mining equipment and tumble-down buildings is a very special kind of 'walkies'.

TUCKER BOX

PIONEER MONUMENT

GUNDAGAI

A TRIBUTE TO OUR PIONEERS.

— UNVEILED BY —

THE. RT. HON. J. A. LYONS. P. C

PRIME MINISTER OF THE

COMMONWEALTH.

28-11-1932.

Northern Territory

Mindil Beach Sunset Markets

Running from April to October, the sights and smells of Darwin's multicultural markets will be enough to give your dog whiplash as it tries to take in all the Asian food stalls, arts and crafts and street performers. The market now has over 200 stalls and you just grab your favourite food and head down to the beach to watch the sun disappear.

mindil.com.au

Darwin Ski Club

Another place that gets ready every night to salute the sunset is the Darwin Ski Club, just opposite the Museum and Art Gallery of the Northern Territory. Dogs and their owners are permitted out on the lawn, which takes the best advantage of the harbourside location. A Darwin classic.

darwinskiclub.com.au

Crazy Acres Mango Farm, Berry Springs

Also open seasonally, Crazy Acres uses the Kensington Pride mango grown on the property for a range of snacks from the mango and banana smoothie bowl to pulled pork rolls, platters, salads and mango cheesecake or homemade ice cream.

You can take your dog on a wander around the grounds and enjoy the rows of mango trees.

crazyacres.com.au

Marlow Lagoon, Darwin

This is not your average suburban dog park, with 31,000 square metres of parkland, barbecue facilities, a huge lagoon to swim in (at the right times of year), a fully equipped obstacle course and extensive off-lead section.
palmerston.nt.gov.au

Black Russian Caravan Cafe, Katherine

One of the best places to refuel with indulgent toasties like a cheesy chipotle chicken with grilled onion and triple cheddar or the haloumi stack with pickled peppers, sun-dried tomatoes, pesto and cheddar. You can park your pup near the van and have the best thing you will find between two slices of bread.
facebook.com/theblackrussiancaravanbar

Erldunda Roadhouse

More than just a place to sleep or refuel, this Red Centre roadhouse offers home cooking, accommodation, caravan park, a pool and even an emu farm. The roadhouse is a great base for exploring Uluru and Kata Tjuta and is located at the intersection of the Stuart Highway and the Lasseter Highway; quite a few options for doggy dining and staying the night.
erldundaroadhouse.com

Queensland

SUP with your pup

Hit the warm Queensland waters with a stand-up paddleboard lesson with your dog. Most SUP operators, such as Enviro Reefs Paddle and Surf School in Bargara, will allow you to take your dog for a try out. And, who knows, you might wind up hanging paw at the Dog Surfing Championships held during the Noosa Festival of Surfing each year in May.
noosafestivalofsurfing.com

Eat Street Northshore, Brisbane

A weekly open-air party with music, shopping, food, drink and

entertainment, the Eat Street district operates every Friday, Saturday and Sunday. Pets are welcome as long as they abide by a few rules of being on a short lead, steering clear of food prep areas and making sure they do not stray onto the fake grass.
eatstreetnorthshore.com.au

Farmers Markets, Brisbane

The various markets in Brisbane and beyond are a great place to take your dog. Markets like the renamed West End Markets in Davies Park offer incredible produce and pooch-friendly picnics under a huge canopy of fig trees and loads of stalls from fashion to healthy snacks.
daviesparkmarket.com.au

Yatala Drive-in

Take your dog to the movies at the Yatala drive-in theatre south of Brisbane. The menu here, for humans anyway, is retro American diner and your dog won't be the only dog on the premises; there are chilli dogs, cheese and bacon dogs and standard hot dogs, or for a big appetite try the Elvis beef and cheeseburger.

fivestarcinemas.com.au

Kangaroo Point Stair Climb, Brisbane

Popular with runners who like to post their Strava times online, this epic stair climb is also a great one to do with your dog, if you both have the stamina. You will both be worn out after this ascent but will be rewarded with great views across the Brisbane CBD.

South Bank, Brisbane

Keep an eye on the events at this open-air riverside precinct in Brisbane with 17 hectares of parkland. Pets are allowed at most of the festivals and events, as well as a few of the cafes with a view.

The Spit, Noosa

Year-round off lead access to a sparkling spot on the Noosa River where you can join picnickers watching the world go by.

Magnetic Island

Pack a muzzle as your pet will need it on the ferry ride, but otherwise you are free to roam the impossible boulders and military history of Magnetic Island just off the coast of Townsville. Just watch the signs as half of 'Maggie' is national park and therefore off limits.

visitmagneticisland.com.au

All Paws Paradise, Gold Coast

Get your pup surf ready with the Aqua Dog Jetty Jump experience at Pimpana. Based on a US experience, this is like a long jump for dogs where the landing is a very soft aquatic one. Encourage your dog to run the full length of the jetty and let fly – they will have a ball.

allpawsparadise.com

Tasmania

Salamanca Market

Salamanca Market is Tassie produce at its finest and it offers the unique option of RSPCA Puppy Parking, which is staffed by volunteers to care for your canines while you shop; made possible with a small donation.
salamancamarket.com.au

Port Arthur Historic Site

Revolving around the prison colony of Port Arthur, this place is often portrayed as hell on earth, but it was also one of the first places in the British Empire to attempt to rehabilitate its prisoners, and the old buildings are wonderfully preserved to bring the story to life. Dogs are not only allowed but have their own entrance to avoid going through the visitor centre.
portarthur.org.au

Tahune AirWalk, Geeveston

Want to find out if your dog is scared of heights? Test your mutt's mettle on the Tahune AirWalk, a metal walkway suspended 30 metres above the forest floor with the final stretch a full 50 metres above a beautiful bend of the Huon River.

tahuneadventures.com.au

Set sail on the Yukon, Franklin

The *Yukon* is a traditionally built Danish sailing ketch that does tours of Bruny Island or a simple 90-minute calm water cruise. Well-behaved pooches are allowed but call ahead to check.

yukon-tours.com.au

Art Farm, Burchs Bay

This farm is packed full of outdoor sculptures with trails for you and your dog to wander like an outdoor gallery. The works are constantly updated, with an annual exhibition, and guests are encouraged to BYO picnics as there is no catering onsite.

artfarmbirchsbay.org.au

Darlington Vineyard, Orford

This cellar door already has a killer view across to Maria Island and has over 5000 vines including the classic Tassie pinot noir, chardonnay, riesling and sauvignon blanc. Dogs are free to wander the vines on-lead and the vineyard is not far from Prosser Bay on the Freycinet coast.

darlingtonvineyard.com.au

Delish Fine Foods, Burnie

Celebrating Tasmania's incredible produce, this cafe, deli and caterer will give you a taste of Tasmania on the outside deck, with tie-up posts for your furry friend. You can feast on locally farmed salmon, artisan breads and free-range eggs all on the incredible Cradle Coast.

Bridestowe Lavender Farm, Nabowla

This is the largest privately owned lavender farm in the world at 260 acres and gives you plenty of options to roam through the rows of purple flowers and open spaces on the farm. There is also a store on

the farm where you can buy a range of products that all use true French lavender, *Lavandula angustifolia*, the only lavender variety suitable for use in perfume and cooking.
bridestowelavender.com.au

Sheffield Murals

Combine a walk with some street art on the Sheffield Mural Tour. What started as a modest way to promote the town back in 1986 has grown to over 200 outdoor murals making the town one of the most extensive outdoor art galleries in the country.
sheffieldtasmania.com.au

Willie Smith's Apple Shed, Huon Valley

Learn about the fruit that gave the Apple Isle its name at the Apple Shed, the home of the Willie Smith's cider and host to festivals, gigs and some incredible Tasmanian produce. Dogs are welcome at the outdoor tables and owners will love the seasonal menu that is always different but always delicious.
williesmiths.com.au

South Australia

Follow My Lead Dog Trail Adelaide

This is a specially curated walk by the City of Adelaide that allows dog owners to ramble through the city while seeing the sights, and having plenty of dog-friendly stops along the way. There are over 30 places to visit with doggy cafes, dog clothing stores and plenty of bowls and water stops along the way. Check out the full map online.
explore.cityofadelaide.com.au

Gilles at the Grounds Market, Adelaide

This market run out of the Old Brick Dairy at the Adelaide Showgrounds in Wayville describes itself as 'the people's marketplace' and is Adelaide's original fashion and design market. It encourages recycling and sustainability and now includes emerging design, vintage, upcycled, fashion, home, accessories, food, and entertainment.

West Terrace Cemetery, Adelaide

This heritage-listed cemetery might seem like a macabre choice for a walk but it is packed with local history and offers guided and unguided wanders and you can take your pet on a lead. Cruise through the rosemary, oleander and cypress pines and pristine parklands.
aca.sa.gov.au

Adelaide-Himeji Garden, Adelaide

This Japanese-inspired garden fuses two styles – sensui, using water and kare senzui, using sand to invoke water – and is a great place to be outside with your dog but also see something new.
explore.cityofadelaide.com.au

Victor Harbor Farmers' Market

Held every Saturday morning, rain, hail or shine at Grosvenor Gardens. As well as local produce there are live music and activities for the kids. There is plenty of space to sit and sample your purchases.
victorharborfarmersmarket.com.au

Victoria

Truffle hunts

Does your dog have what it takes to be a truffle dog? Find out with the curated dog-friendly tour from Gourmet Pawprints that starts with a sniffing lesson at Port Melbourne before heading off to look for this most decadent of ingredients.
gourmetpawprints.com.au

Urban Explorer

Also by the Gourmet Pawprints team, this tour offers a Fido-friendly cruise down the Yarra River as part of a 4-kilometre wander in the city and, being Melbourne, it ends in a bar.
gourmetpawprints.com.au

Take a Punt, Botanic Gardens, Melbourne

A guided punting tour on the Ornamental Lake in the Royal Botanic Gardens in Melbourne is a fun afternoon for you and your dog.

Then you can wander the gardens with your pet (on lead) or have a high tea in the cafe.
puntingonthelake.com.au

Welcome to Thornbury
This food truck park in the northern suburbs has a rotating stable of four-wheeled kitchens and plenty of room for four-legged companions. Keep an eye on the website for trivia nights and local festivals.
welcometothornbury.com

The Pet Grocer
A holistic, raw food store for the pampered pets in Melbourne's southern suburbs. Take your dog for a browse for some seriously high-end treats – perhaps one of the seasonal boxes with 100 per cent natural snacks from Australia and New Zealand – and 'apothecary' like cleansing bars and calming solutions.
thepetgrocer.com

Cannibal Creek Winery, Gippsland

Want to pretend that your pet is a 'wine dog' for the day? Head out to Cannibal Creek in Gippsland, a family-run, pet-friendly operation where you can wander in the bush and finish up with a lunch packed with incredible regional produce.

cannibalcreek.com.au

Have a Snow Day, High Country

Based in Botanic Ridge in the Victorian High Country, Puppy Tales Photography offers travellers the chance to stay in pup-friendly accommodation and then get their dog's photo taken in the snow, or simply have a day out with the team and stay wherever you like.

puppytales.com.au

Stay on a Houseboat on the Murray, Mildura

Cruise the Murray River on one of the stately riverboats and with your pet, docking at the pet-friendly pubs and river walks on the banks of the mighty river. Mildura Houseboats offers a pet-friendly range of floating accommodation with spas and a top-deck for taking in the sun. Check them out for a different kind of holiday with pets.

mildurahouseboats.com.au

Cactus Country, Strathmerton

This striking desert landscape has become something of an Instagram sensation with its curated take on the arid Australian landscape. Take your dog for a walk amongst the more than 4000 species of succulents on the 12 acres of sandy walking tracks, then finish up with a cooling cactus ice cream.

cactuscountry.com.au

Australian Kelpie Centre, Casterton

Take your dog, whatever its breed, on the Kelpie Walking Trail in Casterton, the birthplace of this popular local breed. Your tour ends at the Henty Street interpretation centre with a detailed history of the Kelpie.

castertonkelpieassociation.com.au

Take to the Sky in the Yarra Valley

Taking off from Lilydale Airport, Yarra Valley Aviation will happily give your dog a bird's-eye view of the famous wineries and cute townships of the Yarra region. No check in, no queuing, and your own private lounge – show your doggy the high life.

yvaviation.com.au

Western Australia

Kings Park, Perth

Kings Park is one of the world's largest and most beautiful inner-city parks and has a rich Aboriginal and European history, contemporary culture and offers innovative design, displays and services. Kings Park is home to the Western Australian Botanic Garden and has great views back across to the Perth CBD; the garden has over 3000 species of the unique flora of the west.

bgpa.wa.gov.au

See the Monkey Mia Dolphins

Perfect Nature Cruises are one of the rare sailing operators that will allow you to bring your dog along. You need to call ahead and check as dogs are not suitable for all cruises but the team here are happy to take pups

out on the 18-metre catamaran to see the area's famous wildlife. Just hope they have their sea paws!
perfectnaturecruises.com.au

Union Kitchen, Mindarie

Perth is all about the water and this cafe has a great spot on the Mindarie Marina, on the northern outskirts of Perth. Now, there is dog-friendly, and there is a completely separate dog menu with treats like stinky cheese K9 cookies and a lactose-free 'muttshake', or go all out and get a Dogs Bark-fast, the full English of sausage, bacon and scrambled eggs with liver sprinkles. Great distraction while you enjoy the marina life. They also include a Doggie Wall of Fame, and choose pups to feature each month on their wall.
unionkitchen.com.au

Catch a Gig in Broome

The Broome Courthouse Markets are on Saturday but if you want to rock out with your cocker spaniel you need to go to the Thursday Night Markets where there is a host of local live music in the Town Beach Precinct on Hammersley Street. Or for a special market wait for the full-moon-only Staircase to the Moon Markets on the same spot.
broomemarkets.com.au

Tour the Margaret River Vineyards

This special region where sand meets vine is known for its tipples but also for its amazing produce and the annual food festival that celebrates talented chefs from the region and around the world. You can have a perfectly curated, dog-friendly visit to the region with Grape Escape South West Tours, a boutique winery tour that was the first and only dog-friendly tour operator running 'Pawesome Private Tours' in the region.
grapeescapewa.com.au

The Beach Shack, Exmouth

This joint serves up buckets of mussels and prawns right on the sand at Bundegi Beach where the sand forms part of the outdoor section where you can sit with your dog. You can choose whether you catch the sunrise with a Shack Eggs Benni, or a sunset with a cold beer in hand.
facebook.com/beachshackexmouth

Lake Monger, Wembley

Get a side order of local First Nations' history with your walk at this lake that has historical ties to the Noongar people. Check out the interpretative plaques around the 3.5-kilometre loop track that circles the lake.
cambridge.wa.gov.au

Great Southern Distilling Company, Albany

This group owns three distilleries, two under the Great Southern Distilling Co banner and one distillery operates under the brand Margaret River Distilling Co. They have all been producing award-

winning Australian whisky and gin for more than 15 years and dogs are welcome while you try some of the top-notch drops.
distillery.com.au

Clancy's Fish Pub

The colourful interiors of this small chain of pubs in the west have been welcoming pubgoers and their pups for more than 30 years. There are four branches, in Fremantle, Canning Bridge, City Beach and Dunsborough, all with outdoor seating, perfect for you and your pup.
clancysfishpub.com.au

Visit Swan Valley

The Swan Valley winery region is a must-visit when you are out west and there is a huge range of wineries, breweries and cafes that cater to those travelling with dogs. Head to the Swan Valley information centre and they will help you plan out a doggy-tolerant trip.
swanvalley.com.au

CHAPTER EIGHT

EATING AND DRINKING

E

Throw me a bone here: a round-up of the best dog-friendly cafes

With the explosion of pet ownership post-COVID, dog owners are more than just tolerated at cafes these days, their dogs are actually catered for. Many places have actually worked out that dogs are good for business. People will come more often if they can bring their pets and if their dog is an Insta celeb the venue will often get more engagement from photos of dogs at their cafes than they do of people.

'"Dog-friendly" for many cafes just means there is a bowl of water out front,' says Manny Capones, owner of Collingwood's Doghouse Dog Cafe. 'Anyone can be dog-friendly but we have taken it to the next level.'

Capones is passionate about a raw-food diet for dogs and that forms part of the ethos of the cafe but he also wants the space to be more than just dogs sitting under tables on a lead. The outdoor area is off-lead and they encourage dog birthdays, host doggy dinners and have a range of impressive treats including Pawroni and Paw Blonde doggy beers.

The Pawroni is chicken-stock based and includes glucosamine, MSM and chondroitin so it is a 'bit of fun but there is a benefit behind it'. The beer is recommended to be poured over kibble to liven things up or can be frozen into ice blocks to flavour water.

Also known as the Pupcake Man, Capones has been a chef for 20 years and he now brings his skills to dog treats in the form of small, cooked cakes for canines.

'We started off at markets and it just went crazy,' he says. 'It's all good nutrition, that is behind everything we do, there are a lot of good things in there. We use human-grade products but also try to make it affordable for everyone.'

The dog cafe was inspired by Capone's German shepherd, Luna, now sadly deceased, but they have a new feisty shepherd pup called Axl. Outside in the cafe the dogs can have fun with other pups but there are also sectioned off booths for the humans away from the canine chaos, and if your dog is a resource guarder they can pop into the booth and have their pupcake to themselves.

'We do special events, so we are now doing ramen bowls for dogs and we do little sushi plates,' Capones says. 'Anyone can do a dog-uccino or a treat so we have gone an extra couple of steps and upped the ante.'

This includes deliveries of raw food on Wednesdays and Fridays including special health blends for dogs with health conditions. The cafe is a registered pet food supplier and has a pet nutritionist-in-training on staff as well.

'Our first priority is the dog's health and wellbeing and then the fun comes after,' Capones says.

With this level of dog-friendliness in mind, we present a list of some of the most over-the-top cafes where dogs are treated like one of the family.

Australian Capital Territory

The Cupping Room, Canberra

Purveyors of ONA coffee, the largest specialty coffee roaster in the ACT, the Cupping Room was designed as a place to share coffee knowledge. The name stems from the term 'cupping' which is the technique of comparing coffees. It will all be over your dear dog's head, but they are welcome to tag along.
thecuppingroom.com.au

Eat Me Drink Me, Kaleen

There are pups aplenty at this Alice in Wonderland-inspired cafe in the Canberra suburbs that is open bright and early for those on an early morning exercise stroll.
facebook.com/eatmedrinkmecanberra

Bittersweet, Kingston

Kingston is a pretty pup-friendly burb anyway with plenty of paths to take beside the lake, but a pit stop at Bittersweet is well worth it for the great food and coffee made with care.
facebook.com/bittersweet.act

Local Press Cafe, Kingston

Another great place to refuel on the Kingston Foreshore is Local Press that has a strong health and wholefoods bent. Sit outside on the multicoloured wooden chairs and enjoy a coffee and a snack that you won't have to feel guilty about.
localpresscafe.com.au

Millhouse Cafe, Queanbeyan

Housed in a storybook beautiful cottage, with a kids' playhouse and slides at the rear, there is plenty of garden available for dogs to make themselves at home. A huge tree dominates the outdoor area and the coffee and food is on point. It might technically be across the border, but it's only a short trip from Canberra.
millhousecafe.com.au

New South Wales

The Grounds of Alexandria, Alexandria

This sprawling inner-city cafe is a combo of cafe, garden (including a potting shed) and bar, but pups will need to be used to being around lots of people as, while the space is big, it is always heaving with fans of the food, coffee and atmosphere here. Keep an eye out for the regular high teas.
thegrounds.com.au

Treehouse on Belongil, Belongil Beach

Right on Belongil Beach, this waterside coffee spot is an all-day affair with a brekky menu, woodfired pizzas for lunch and cocktails when the sun goes down. There is even live music of an evening and pups are welcome to visit at all times if they are under control and well behaved.
treehouseonbelongil.com

The Downward Dog Co, Bodalla

This is a community space offering music, art, and activities for the south coast locals. But they also have 'pooch pampering' that befits the cafe's name where you will find dog beds, dog biscuits and puppuccinos.
downwarddogcafe.com.au

Porch and Parlour, Bondi Beach

This cafe is no COVID convert having served local pups for over a decade, and it is back after a recent renovation. Doggies are welcome on the 'porch' part with great views over Sydney's famous stretch of sand.
porchandparlour.com

Sprout, Eden

You and your dog can have a whale of a time at this cafe and local produce store with a secret garden out back just built for lounging around in. The cafe is committed to supporting local growers and to reducing food miles, the menu is seasonal and the welcome warm.
sprouteden.com.au

Dachshund Coffee, Hunters Hill

You would hope that a coffee brand named after a dog would allow for canine customers and you would be right. There is a sustainable, plant-based bent to this popular caff, rumoured to have one of the best smashed avos in a city obsessed with this destroyer of house deposits.
dachshundcoffee.com

The Grumpy Baker

This fast-growing chain of spectacular sourdough welcomes pups across all its venues but we have a soft spot for the Vaucluse outpost as it is just a short walk from the stunning coastline of The Gap and Watsons Bay

(though pooches are not allowed on much of the sand here so keep an eye out for signs).
thegrumpybaker.com.au

Cafe Bones, Leichhardt
This outdoor cafe in the middle of the Hawthorne Canal dog park bills itself as the world's first dog-friendly cafe, and while this is sure to spark some debate due to the enormity of the claim, there is little argument about how dog-friendly it is today. It is a great spot in the sun and also has a range of merchandise like mugs painted with all your furry friends.
facebook.com/cafebones

Northern Territory

Ray's Cafe and Patisserie, Darwin
Truffled scrambled eggs in a tropical plant-lined courtyard in the capital of the Top End. That alone sounds perfect but they are dog-friendly to boot.
facebook.com/rayspatisserieandcafe

The Boatshed, Darwin

Sea breezes and a stack of Nutella crepes are on offer at this bayside cafe in Cullen Bay that allows dogs out on the deck. From here you can ogle all the high-end watercraft in the marina and enjoy one hell of a sunrise or sunset.

facebook.com/boatshedcoffeehouse

Eva's Cafe, Darwin Botanic Gardens

Inside a heritage-listed Wesleyan church surrounded by the lush Darwin Botanic Gardens you can wander one of the tree-lined trails and then break for a coffee with your dog at your side.

botanicgardenscafe.com.au

De La Plage, Darwin

This family- and dog-friendly cafe spills out onto the Casuarina Coastal Reserve where you can pull up a colourful beanbag, hammock or umbrella to go with your freshly brewed cup of wake-up juice.

delaplagecafe.com.au

Queensland

Barkley and Pips, Bundamba

This over-the-top dog cafe might serve you up some dog treats lovingly shaped to look like mini pizza slices, or a whole tray full of doggy canapés. Dogs are their business as the cafe is attached to a doggy boutique that sells a range of upmarket haute pup-ture.

facebook.com/barkleyandpips

Wharf One, Cairns

This waterfront cafe is a Cairns classic and you can catch a great breakfast, water views and sea breezes with you dog here. They advertise themselves cutely as 'pet-friendly for friendly pets' but this is one of the great spots in Cairns to experience the coast and still have your pet by your side.

wharfonecafe.com.au

Brother Jenkins, Cairns

This cafe, just north of the centre of town in Mununda, not only welcomes dogs but they can be serenaded at some of the regular gigs. It's a sustainable place that likes you to bring your own cup if you can but they always have water on hand for your dog.
facebook.com/brotherjenkinscafe

Dune Cafe, Currumbin Lagoon

Just next to the great walking spot that is Palm Beach Parklands and overlooking the stunning lagoon, this cafe is a great spot to stop for a post-walk cuppa.
dunecafe.com.au

Coco Havana, Indooroopilly

Decked out as exotically as it sounds – fairy lights, succulents, mismatched chairs and your grandma's plates – this garden cafe has plenty of space for your dog to stretch out. Amazing gelato flavours too: try the almond and quandong.
cocohavana.com.au

Frida Kahlo's Summer House, Kangaroo Point

A riot of colour and Mexican flavours that has a big, shaded courtyard for pups and is licensed, if you would like a cheeky afternoon beer or wine. Or if you are really adventurous try a michelada (beer, lime and juice).
fksh.com.au

Murray's, Maroochydore

Another place that loves its pooches enough to have a special menu for them so, if they are not worn out from a walk, they at least have food to keep them busy while the humans feast on some of the fresh-baked treats Murray's is known for.

murrayscafe.com.au

Poets Cafe, Montville

Looking like it has got lost on the way to Europe, this elegant cafe has plenty of gardens for dogs to lounge in while their owners try the signature drink, a not-so-humble coffee that is made from spring water that bubbles away beneath the cafe itself.

poetscafe.com.au

Todd & Pup, Moorooka

Ahead of the pack when it comes to its treatment of brunch dogs (they're a thing, I just called it) is Todd & Pup. There are dog menus, a dog hashtag (#dogsoftoddandpup) and a huge mural of the romantic spaghetti scene from *Lady and the Tramp*.

facebook.com/toddandpup

Brown Dog Cafe, Woolloongabba

The clue is in the name at this very dog-friendly brekky spot that has even named some of its dishes like the Big Dog's Breakfast after their furry patrons, so you know they are going to give your fur baby the full treatment.

browndogcafe.cafeleader.com

South Australia

Octeine Coffee, Adelaide

If you have an adventure-loving pupster they will be welcome at this coffee shop from the adventure and outdoors brand Octeine, with options in the Adelaide CBD and out at Seppeltsfield. The coffee is obsessively roasted in house.

octeine.com.au

Boy & Bloom, Adelaide

This is another cafe that wears its love of all things dog on its socials with plenty of paws on display on Facebook and Instagram. Dog owners are known to order a side of extra bacon especially for you-know-who at this centrally located venue.

facebook.com/BoyandBloom

Peter Rabbit, Adelaide

A quirky cafe that looks like it is situated in the fictional Mr McGregor's garden, there are no bunnies here to distract the legion of dogs that love dozing in the shade. Coffee is the dominant passion but a love of seasonal produce is a close second.

peterabbit.com.au

Dear Daisy, Adelaide

This Forestville cafe's love of dogs is written all over the wall in a stupendously large mural. The breakfast burrito is a much-loved favourite but so too are the smoothies (chocolate, banana and peanut butter to be exact) and baked goods.

facebook.com/deardaisycafe

Pavé Cafe, Adelaide

A riot of recycled timber and greenery, Pavé in Norwood is a very inviting spot to share a puppuccino with your cafe-loving canine. They also do a great, and very speedy, takeaway service if you are just passing through on a walk.

pavecafe.com.au

Whistle and Flute, Adelaide

Part cafe, part liquor bar, all dog-friendly, this is the place to while away a lazy afternoon in Unley with a vegan falafel bowl and a glass of Adelaide wine from not very far away.

whistleandflute.com.au

The Ripple & Swirl, Christies Beach

A lovely beachside cafe on the Fleurieu Peninsula, The Ripple & Swirl is a spot beloved by locals and the dogs who love them. Simple, sunny day

food and great coffee with views of the ocean.
facebook.com/therippleandswirl

Oxenberry Farm, McLaren Vale

The huge paved deck at this winery cafe is ideal for some wine tasting with your dog and you can grab a huge lunch platter or a cheeky afternoon gelato. You are at the start of the Shiraz Trail if you fancy wandering further afield.
oxenberry.com

The Golden Fleece, Willunga

This retro cafe is all about the baking with strawberry and dark chocolate muffins, white chocolate macadamia biscuits and a special range of dog treats on offer for your companion.
facebook.com/thegoldenfleececafe

Barista Sister, Nuriootpa (Barossa Valley)

This Barossa Valley cafe is for those who take their coffee seriously. They roast their organic coffee beans onsite and specialise in alternate brewing methods such as cold brew and V60 pour over. There are shaded tables out the front where you can enjoy a coffee with your furry friend as well as a cute dog-friendly laneway.
facebook.com/BaristaSistaBeanery

Tasmania

Room for a Pony, Hobart

Room for a pony, plenty of room for a dog at this friendly space that has its own hashtag to celebrate visiting doggos (#dogsofthepony). Try the huevos rancheros with local sourdough.
roomforapony.com.au

Hamlet, Hobart

Hamlet thrives on its strong connection to the local community and it is a social enterprise cafe helping to tackle unemployment in Tassie. This social conscience also means that your dogs are very welcome;

they are part of your family and part of the Hamlet family as well.
hamlet.org.au

Giddy Up Foodstore, Hobart

You will find Tassie's cafe-going canines all over the Facebook feed of this cafe in Sandy Bay. Dogs are welcome in the sunny courtyard, and the kitchen turns out some of the best brunches on the Apple Isle.
facebook.com/giddyup.foodstore

The Cornelian Boathouse, Hobart

You can sit at this cafe and restaurant by the waterfront in Cornelian Bay with your dog or grab some seafood chowder or battered flathead from the takeaway menu and take a stroll around the bay.
theboathouse.com.au

Ginger Brown, Hobart

This incredible lunch spot will have humans panting to get their hands on such fare as a chilli and lemongrass braised brisket on a bagel with a fried egg and chipotle mayo, bean shoots and spring onion. And it is near the Washington Street off-lead dog area for a wander afterwards.
facebook.com/gingerbrownhobart

Liberty Coffee, Launceston

This cute cafe has limited outdoor seating but a big love of pets, and will pop out a table whatever the weather to accommodate furry friends. The seats have a view of the historic Central Methodist Church opposite and the coffee is heavenly.
facebook.com/LibCoffee

Earthy Eats, Launceston

This organic and sustainability focused cafe has an amazing breakfast menu from the scrambled tofu to a smoothie bowl with hazelnut granola. They also sell takeaway 'care packages' stuffed full of seasonal vegetables and produce.
earthyeats.com.au

Patchwork Cafe, New Norfolk

Plenty of grass to play on and doggy trampoline beds are just some of the dog-friendly touches at this regional cafe. The coffee regularly features on the 'best in Tassie' lists and the food it top notch.
facebook.com/patchworkcafenn

Victoria

Drive Cafe, Ballarat

Under a metal canopy that once protected petrol pumps, local diners are now filling up on lemon and rhubarb waffles with spiced mascarpone or 'southside' zucchini and corn fritters with tomato jam and Meredith goats cheese. The idea behind Drive was to turn a derelict 'gas and go' into a space for great coffee and community connection, and that includes your pup.
drive-cafe.com

Tiny, Beechworth

This licensed cafe at the base of the Victorian alps not only slings dogs – chilli, New York-style and basic hot dogs – but it welcomes them as well. Go for breakfast or head in for the regular Dog & Grog evenings.
facebook.com/tinybeechworth

The Boardwalk, Bendigo

The cafe mascot dog, Chino the chocolate Lab, welcomes his fellow canines to this regional cafe which has a specially dedicated doggy menu curated by K9 Catering. Humans will have to make do with a smoothie bowl or Bircher muesli.
theboardwalkbendigo.com.au

Long Paddock, Lindenow

In an unassuming main street in Lindenow next to a vintage Caltex service station, Long Paddock is just as comfortable serving doorstop-sized cakes to locals as it is wowing foodie travellers with a degustation that might include Merimbula rock oysters with finger lime mignonette on Seasalt Bakery rye or gnocchi with Lakes Entrance school prawns, tomato and nduja.
longpaddock.com.au

Jardin Tan, Melbourne

This outdoor coffee spot is at the entrance to the Royal Botanic Gardens and right on the popular 'Tan Track' for walking dogs and going for a run. It is the perfect place to take your pet before or after a wander around the sights, sounds and smells of the garden itself.
jardintan.com.au

West Beach Pavilion, Melbourne
Sit right on sand, and right next to an off-lead dog beach, at this historic St Kilda pavilion on the popular city beach. They even do a selection of beach picnic baskets if you want to have an even more secluded sandy lunch with your four-legged friend.
westbeachstkilda.com.au

Lux Foundry, Melbourne
Housed in the historic Brunswick Gas and Coke Company building from 1889 this brick space is now a modern cafe with a big courtyard and a love for dogs. Pups can be seen on their website and if yours is cute enough it might just make a guest appearance on the Lux Instagram account. The food and coffee are top notch too.
luxfoundry.com.au

The Winey Cow, Mornington

This cafe on the peninsula, with a side of wine and cocktails, is so keen to engage dog owners that they have a dedicated treats menu. You will see plenty of pampered Mornington pooches lapping up the attention. thewineycow.com.au

Bomboras, Torquay

This beach-shack-chic joint has a menu that follows the sun as surfers grab sunrise coffees, date-nighters have cocktails at a pop-up sunset cocktail bar or families settle into the pet-friendly garden on a dog day afternoon. Try a slow-braised honey mustard lamb salad or 'Shipsterns' pizza swimming with prawns, barramundi and roast garlic. bomboras.com.au

Western Australia

Dylans on the Terrace Restaurant and Cafe, Albany

Located in a historic building with views over Albany's Princess Royal Harbour, the menu caters for all tastes, ages and occasions and the homemade cakes are popular. There are dog-friendly tables out the front where you and your pooch can admire the water views.
www.dylans.com.au

Green Mango Cafe, Broome

This cafe turns a little spicy at lunchtime with curries and vegie samosas. And they always have room for a dog or two in the outdoor areas.
facebook.com/greenmangobroome

The Zookeeper's Store, Broome

Not a cage in sight but The Zookeeper's Store is the perfect Cable Beach spot to drop in for something to eat and drink after a stroll, or a swim, at Broome's most famous stretch of stand.
zks.com.au

White Elephant Cafe, Gnarabup

This idyllic Margaret River cafe is the perfect spot for both you and your dog. It is right on the dog beach in Gnarabup and you can grab a takeaway while your dog lets off steam on the beach, or relax under the shady umbrellas on the deck overlooking the ocean.

Sidekick Cafe, Margaret River

Right on the main street of Margaret River township this is another venue for coffee connoisseurs, and their four-legged friends. The coffee options include pour over and cold drip made from freshly roasted single-origin beans. There are also healthy treats (including gluten free), and even dog treats for your good boy or girl.
www.instagram.com/sidekickcafemargs

Little Stove Cafe, Perth

This Bicton cafe is the sort of local you might move house to be near, with artisan dog treats at the counter and a genuine affection

for four-pawed guests. Open for breakfast and lunch you can see the beautiful plating on their Instagram page.
littlestove.com

Yelo, Perth
This beachfront cafe and corner store in Trigg has a verandah literally packed with every man, woman and their dogs. The building was run-down when the owners first took it on and now it functions as a centre for the local community, and their pets. Once you've had your coffee, you can head across the road to the Trigg dog beach.
yelocornerstore.com.au

Sistas, Perth
Formerly known as the Burns Beach Cafe, this is still a dog-friendly joint where you can park your pooch near the sand. They are very upfront about their love of furry friends so head down the beach and find them – it's hard to miss the giant squid mural on the side of the building.
facebook.com/sistas.burns.beach

Sparrow's Nest, Perth
Named after the very social bird, you will also find a whole bunch of dogs hanging out in East Victoria Park with their caffeine-loving owners; or as the cafe itself puts it: 'coffee and dogs really make life complete'.

They are a quaint hideout located away from the hustle and bustle, on the fringe of Vic Park's busy café strip. This intimate sanctuary is lined with mouth watering treats to suit any palate and provides a niche where conversation flows as smoothly as their rich, aromatic coffee.
facebook.com/TheSparrowsNestCafe

PUPPY
HYDRATION
STATION

The
Sparrow's
Nest

The
Sparrow's
Nest
GREAT COFFEE
SWEETS
PABLO

The
Sparrow's
Nest
GREAT COFFEE

Who let the dogs shout?

Quench your thirst at a dog-friendly boozer

I don't know about you but even before I tracked down my Old English sheepdog pup I imagined it lounging under the table in my local pub. The idea of a sunny afternoon, a pint and my furry friend is part of the reason I wanted a dog. But then again I like going to the pub with mates, even the four-legged variety.

In the UK you are likely to spill an ale or two as you trip over a tail or hind leg, so littered are the tavern floors with reclining dogs, but in Australia they are mostly stuck outside. However, there are a few places that are more dog-friendly than others.

Bianca Sondakh has made a business out of finding Melbourne's best dog-friendly places for a beer or wine with her Puppy Pub Crawls (facebook.com/crawlpuppypub). Each week Sondakh and her pugalier (pug and Kings Charles Cavalier cross) Hugo lead a group of hoppy hounds and their owners on a wander between pubs that love dogs.

The business started with a spontaneous night out where Sondakh had Hugo in tow and she began to realise that some places really do go the extra mile for dog owners. So she started her official crawls and raised the bar even further.

'I started asking the bars to make something special for the dogs,' Sondakh says. 'And now we have dog martinis on all the crawls, we have had doggy pizzas and doggy beers in the past and we have a little doggy meal on some crawls as well.'

Obviously, the doggy martinis are not alcoholic but they are appealing to the dogs – things like beef brisket, chicken broth or a mix of fruit juices like carrot, blueberry and banana.

'It is a lot of fun for the people and for the dogs as well,' she says. 'If people just go to the bar on their own with a dog, the dogs do not get their own drink, so my favourite time is always when they are having their treats. And the dogs get to play with other dogs, the people get to socialise and the dogs do as well.'

Most bars give the crawls their own space outside, so the pups can sometimes go off-lead. The puppy pub crawls can skew female except for when Sondakh includes breweries in the mix, which brings the blokes out, and they tend to be locals who come out with their dogs for a look at what their suburb has to offer. The crawls post which suburb they will be taking place in on Facebook and they often sell out, so it is a good idea to book early, particularly if you are on a holiday trip from another state.

We took a recent crawl around the Melbourne suburb of Brunswick, starting at the Edinburgh Castle, and it was clear from the outset that it was not just the humans that were going to have fun on this sunny Sunday afternoon.

The crawl kicks off with introductions, where owners talk a bit about themselves and their pooch. The dogs ranged from an aging rescue greyhound to an 11-week-old cavoodle, while Hugo wandered around sniffing butts like a seasoned professional.

From the Edinburgh Castle the crew took a wander down busy Sydney Road to the Retreat Hotel, a Brunswick live music institution with a beer garden dominated by a huge tree. Strains of local balladeer Charles Jenkins came out of the bandroom as we walked our dogs around to the beer garden, where a tray of doggy martinis was awaiting us. Overflowing with pulled beef brisket, the dogs wolfed their 'drinks' down like the first beer after a long week at work while the owners grabbed another round and chatted while madly untangling leads.

The final stop was the food truck park Welcome to Brunswick with a bar run by Sydney-based brewer Four Pines. There was a special stall set up by Collingwood's Doghouse Dog Cafe where the dogs were treated to a meaty 'pupcake' and the humans ordered plates of loaded fries from the Mr Burger food truck. Then it was time for goodbyes and it was hard to say who was harder to get moving home, the owners or the dogs.

To help with a pup crawl of your own, we have assembled some of the most dog-accepting drinking holes across Australia.

Australian Capital Territory

Assembly, Braddon

Known as the 'people's pub', this Braddon boozer has one of the best beer gardens in the ACT with space, heaters in winter, and a tinnie bar that means you don't have to stray too far from your dog to grab another round.

thepeoplespub.com.au

Bentspoke Brewing Co, Braddon

This brew-pub is dog-friendly at the outside tables but be prepared for a wait as they are prime real estate. But when you do snag one make sure you stay for lunch as their chicken burger might well be one of the best things to come between two slices of bread. Check the chalkboard for some special brews and make sure you head upstairs to have a look at the tanks and brewery that make it all possible.

bentspokebrewing.com.au

The Old Canberra Inn, Lyneham

This inn is certainly old, with roots going back to 1857 when it first welcomed drinkers, one of the earliest licensed pubs in the region to do so. What started as a slab hut is now a modern establishment with craft beers and a mod-Oz pub menu. Share some history with your hooch-loving hound.

oldcanberrainn.com.au

George Harcourt Inn, Nicholls

The courtyard of the George Harcourt is a lovely spot for dogs and their humans to unwind on the rows of trestle tables out in the sun. Go during the week for the midweek special lunches when things get a bit more interesting.

georgeharcourt.com

New South Wales

Surveyor General Inn, Berrima

This classic sandstone pub in the sleepy Southern Highlands town of Berrima allows frosty puppies to curl up inside in front of the blazing open fire. Outside there are plenty of spots for your dog under the shady terrace and it is just near the Berrima River Walk if you want to burn off your pub lunch.
surveyorgeneralinn.com.au

Bredbo Inn, Bredbo

This pub is a great break for drivers heading to the Snowy Mountains and it loves to stoke a rumour that the Man from Snowy River himself died on the premises after falling from his horses outside. Banjo Patterson was a regular visitor and your dog can be too.
bredboinn.com.au

Beach Hotel, Byron Bay

Overlooking Main Beach, this is one of the most famous beachside pubs in the state and the good news is that you can have your dog in the spacious outdoor area. Head in for some sun, sea and sounds, with gigs in the early evening.
beachhotel.com.au

The Golden Sheaf, Double Bay

The leafy beer garden of this Eastern suburbs hotel has welcomed pampered pooches for decades while their owners have a schooner or two; check out the free-flowing brunch that is a bit of an institution.
thegoldensheaf.com.au

The Erko, Erskineville

The Erko is a friendly neighbourhood pub that is one of the Sydney pubs (and there are a surprising number of them) that are happy for your dog to be inside with you. They have an in-house smoker and some amazing American-style barbecue comes out of it, so if the weather is not very nice you can huddle up with your pup, an open fire and some ribs.
theerko.com.au

Vic on the Park, Marrickville

Another pub that gives dogs free reign over most of the indoor and outdoor areas, the Vic on the Park loves dogs, but it is also a live music venue so check what's on if you have a noise-sensitive pet.
merivale.com/venues/viconthepark

Courthouse Hotel, Newtown

You will find inner-city pups in the sprawling beer garden at 'The Courty' which is a shabby-chic gem that has been unchanged in this boho neighbourhood for years. Come for the footy, a hefty pub meal or to soak up the sun outside. The Courty is one of the best pubs in Sydney, it is really just a bonus that you can take your dog with you.
courthousehotel.com.au

The Newport, Newport

Formerly the Newport Arms, this legendary drinking spot has been given the Merivale treatment of late (having been purchased by the Sydney-based hospitality giant) but the multi-level outdoor area that was a huge draw still welcomes dogs on a lead. The Newport is open all day from smoothie breakfasts through to freshly shucked oysters, so grab an outside seat and enjoy.
merivale.com/venues/thenewport

Silverton Hotel, Silverton

This outback hotel has starred in *Mad Max, Mission: Impossible 2* and Aussie film classic *Wake in Fright*. If you are passing through you simply have to drop in to this piece of film history and bring your pet with you; Max would never leave 'Dog' behind.
silvertonhotel.com.au

Thirsty Crow Brewing Co, Wagga Wagga

Family-owned brew-pub that started in 2011 in the country town of Wagga Wagga, the Crow has plenty of outdoor space for dogs but things can get a bit lively in the evenings so check ahead to make sure there is some space for your pet.
thirstycrow.com.au

Northern Territory

Monte's Lounge, Alice Springs

This large, lively, bohemian tavern also has a beer garden and covered outdoor area where you can hang out with your pooch. The pub-food menu has options for everyone including vegans and there's some sort of entertainment on most nights at this circus-like venue.

monteslounge.com.au

Berry Springs Tavern, Berry Springs

This traditional tavern south of Darwin on the way to Litchfield National Park has the sort of huge outdoor space you expect in the heart of big-sky country and there is a country welcome of a similar size. Break up your road trip with a stop and a cold beer.

berryspringstavern.com

Beachfront Hotel, Darwin

What was a classic Darwin boozer got a major makeover a couple of years back but there is still a huge deck with plenty of room for dogs of all shapes and sizes. The Nightcliff pub hosts live music, does breakfast and has a sports bar for all the major matches.

beachfronthotel.com.au

Monsoons, Darwin

While Monsoons might bill itself as a party spot, you can still take a lazy pooch and enjoy the large outdoor verandah where you can watch the crowds wander along busy Mitchell Street.

monsoonsdarwin.com.au

The Precinct Tavern, Darwin

The Precinct Tavern is situated on the ground level of the Adina Vibe building at the Darwin Waterfront, just a short walk from the wave pool and the Darwin Convention Centre near the Darwin CBD. It is a fantastic spot to hang out during the day or night with uninterrupted views of the Darwin Waterfront.

theprecincttavern.com.au

Queensland

Birdsville Hotel, Birdsville

One of the classic outback pubs, it would be a shame to make it this far along the Birdsville Track and not be able to share a cold beer with a four-legged friend. Pull up a piece of red dirt outside this sandstone pub that dates back to 1884, or grab something from the nearby Birdsville Baker, which is owned by the same crew and also welcomes pets – and keep an eye on the sky as there is a place to park your Cessna nearby for those coming by air.

birdsvillehotel.com.au

Brewdog DogTap, Brisbane

It would stand to reason that Murarrie brewer Brewdog would have a canine-compatible place to enjoy their craft beers. DogTap has 28 taps distributing their Sunshine State brews and the best place for you and your pet to enjoy them is on the sun terrace overlooking the Brisbane River.

brewdog.com/dogtap-brisbane

The Triffid, Brisbane

This bar is owned by Brisbane rock royalty, Powderfinger bassist John 'JC' Collins, and hosts some of the best gigs in town inside the venue. But you can also enjoy a beer and a burger outside in the sunny beer garden of the Newstead venue, which also has the occasional gig.
thetriffid.com.au

Sea Legs Brewing, Brisbane

Another brew house that is welcoming to pets, Sea Legs Brewing has one of the most iconic spots in Brisbane as its sits under the Story Bridge at Kangaroo Point. Bookings are recommended for big groups.
sealegsbrewing.com.au

Kettle & Tin, Brisbane

Bar, cafe, or diner, this foodie spot set in an old Queenslander in Paddington is certainly pup-forward with plenty of places for dogs to lounge under a table while their humans enjoy a mod-Oz menu and a cold beer.
kettleandtin.com.au

Hope & Anchor, Brisbane

Still in the eastern suburb of Paddington, one of the dog-friendliest burbs in Brissie, you can head to this English-inspired 'best little boozer in Paddington' set in an old bakery with pavement seating for you and your dog to spend a lazy Sunday afternoon.
hopeandanchor.net.au

Hemingway's Brewery, Cairns

Housed in a heritage-listed building on the Cairns Wharf, Hemingway's is a great waterside spot for a brew with your brew dog. They love furry friends and if you are in Port Douglas they have another outlet with a similarly welcoming vibe for dog owners, so check that one out as well.
hemingwaysbrewery.com

Brightwaters Hotel, Sunshine Coast

This large Mountain Creek lakeside hotel is a family-friendly spot with multiple spaces and facilities and your fur kids can come along for

the ride. The menu is pub classics leaning heavily on surf and turf using some of the incredible local seafood.
brightwaterhotel.com.au

FOMO Brewing, Sunshine Coast

You can dine all day at this brewhouse on Sunshine Beach. Nightly there is a changing menu to match with the house-brewed drops but if you are an early bird how about foregoing the beers for poached free-range eggs on pumpkin sourdough. This flexible spot is perfect no matter what time of day you arrive.
fomobrewing.com.au

Bar Wunder, Toowoomba

This is one of the dog-friendliest joints in the north with a very clear 'BYO dogs' policy and pictures of their doggy diners all over the website. If you are in town head to Bar Wunder for some pimped pub fare that elevates the humble hot dog to a feast using giant bratwurst, including a meat-free options for the veggies.
barwunder.com.au

South Australia

The Lion Hotel, Adelaide

The Garden Bar is the spot for some serious puppy naps in amongst the high tables and canopy booths of the Lion. The pub also has events like the 'featured winery' which spotlight one of SA's great winemakers with a talk and tasting.
lionhotel.com.au

Little Bang Brewery Company, Adelaide

The taproom at this young Stepney brewer, whose aluminium beer cans are works of art in themselves, is pup-friendly and is a great place to taste their craft beers, a range of local wines, and the Little Bang gin that is brewed in collaboration with distiller Prohibition Liquor.
littlebang.com.au

Malt Shovel Taphouse, Adelaide

Malt Shovel is behind such brews as Brooklyn Brewery, Eumundi Brewery and Byron Bay Brewery and they have the perfect place to try their different beers on the Adelaide waterfront. Located at the Adelaide Festival Centre, look across the river to Adelaide Oval with a pint in one hand and lead in the other at one of the best dog-friendly spots in the city.
maltshoveltaphouse.com.au

Kangaroo Island Spirits, Kangaroo Island

Another pet-friendly purveyor of distilling is this spot on beautiful Kangaroo Island where on-lead doggies can join the humans for a glass of heavily awarded gin. This is a family affair and it shows, from the originality of the products to the welcome at the cellar door.
kispirits.com.au

Bay of Shoals Wines, Kangaroo Island

While you are on the island grab your dog and head over to Bay of Shoals vineyard near Kingscote for a tasting of their award-winning drops that are uniquely influenced by the maritime climate of the island.
bayofshoalswines.com.au

Alpha Box & Dice, McLaren Vale

You might need to book at this popular winery in McLaren Vale that is undertaking the large-scale project of making a different wine style for each letter of the alphabet. Combine a tasting with a wander through the grounds of the winery and treat your hungry hound to a handmade dog biscuit.

alphaboxdice.com

Goodieson Brewery, McLaren Vale

Not far away from Alpha Box & Dice you can grab a brew at this modern cellar door that is also home to a 'lazy red dog' that might greet your own wine-tasting canine. Sit out on the tree-lined terrace with views across the Mt Lofty ranges.

goodiesonbrewery.com.au

Smiling Samoyed Brewery, Myponga

When you have a pair of grinning samoyeds as your mascots you are definitely dog people and visitors' dogs are also welcome at this brewery. The original '12 Paws' of the brewery were Mia, Cooper and Poppet. The current 'ambassa-dogs' are Hoppy and Kent. Myponga is part of the Fleurieu Peninsula, on the way to Kangaroo Island.

smilingsamoyed.com.au

Stanley Bridge Tavern, Verdun

Friendly local pub with a passion for pups where you can enjoy pan-roasted salmon or some rolled pork belly in the beer garden festooned with fairy lights. There are also a range of pub classics – from a chicken schnitty burger to bangers and mash – served in a lovely old-fashioned boozer.

stanleybridgetavern.com

Tasmania

Hotel Bruny, Bruny Island

It is only right that an island pub focuses on the wealth of seafood at its doorstep and you can enjoy it with your dog on the open deck here. It has amazing views of neighbouring Satellite Island, which you can hire all to yourself, but is sadly not accommodating to four-legged island hoppers.

hotelbruny.com.au

The Brick Factory, Hobart

This meticulously made drinking spot, assembled brick-by-brick by its passionate owners, celebrates all things Tassie on its drinks menu, such as spirits like Forty Spotted Gin from Lark Distillery, the birthplace of the Australian distilling revolution.

thebrickfactory.com.au

The Tasmanian Inn, Hobart

The beer garden of this traditional pub, first established in the Tassie capital in 1851, welcomes dogs all year round. For humans, you can enjoy a locally brewed beer or wine and a great pub meal.

tasmanianinn.com.au

The Salty Dog, Kingston Beach

This pub on the beach at Kingston, south of Hobart, is very accommodating to its namesakes, who are very keen on the pub's ice cream and can even settle in for an afternoon of sun-drenched live music on 'Salty Sundays'. An all-round beach pub classic.

facebook.com/TheSaltyDogHotel

Peppermint Bay Hotel, Woodbridge

Just south of Hobart is this majestic, architecturally designed building with soaring glass windows designed to maximise the views over the D'Entrecasteaux Channel and Bruny Island. It has a seasonal menu that focuses on the best of Tasmania. Grab a table for all of you.

peppermintbay.com.au

Victoria

Hop Temple, Ballarat

The mismatched furniture, peeling paint and upcycled junk lights may appear relaxed but the selection of tap and can beers is so well thought out that Melbourne beer fans make day trips to sample the rare kegs on offer. Food is of the beer-sopping variety (pulled pork burgers, ribs and pizza) and there are plenty of water bowls for the hop dogs.
hoptemple.com.au

Red Bluff Brewers, Lakes Entrance

This beer maker out east is pouring classic tropical ales and pilsners out of a corrugated iron shed just outside of Lakes Entrance, the first brewer in this popular seaside town. Red Bluff's range is best sampled onsite when they have food trucks pull up, like The Tank's woodfired pizzas and the Q Shack that slings American barbecue, that you can then sling under the outdoor table to your pooch.
redbluffbrewers.com

Marlo Pub, Gippsland

The sun-drenched deck of this local pub looks out over an estuary where the Snowy River meets Bass Strait and it is the perfect spot to share a plate piled high with the fried tails of local flathead with a furry friend. It's a warm and welcoming joint also known as the 'cray pot' because once you enter it is very hard to leave – and they have the amazing local brew Sailors Grave on tap.
marlohotel.com.au

The Mountain View Hotel, King Valley

Owned by the Pizzini family, who also make top local drops, this Whitfield pub serves hearty Italian meals – think squid ink linguine – by a log fire in winter and in the sun-flecked beer garden in summer. The area's Italian specialties are available at the bar, as are the local brews from King River Brewing.
mvhotel.com.au

Palace Hotel, Melbourne

There is a great community vibe at the Palace Hotel in South Melbourne, presided over by Billy the pub dog, a staffy who is also the pub's logo. So pooches are welcome here in the shady beer garden.

thepalacehotel.com.au

The Edinburgh Castle, Melbourne

This Brunswick neighbourhood pub recently expanded its dog-friendly beer garden to take in the neighbouring car park, so there is plenty of faux grass for your furry friend to sprawl out on. Bowls are everywhere and dogs are more than just allowed, they are welcomed. They are also a regular participant in the Puppy Pub Crawl (see introduction).

edinburghcastle.net.au

Little Hop, Melbourne

The perfect union of craft beer and tacos on Brunswick Street, Fitzroy is a great incentive for dog owners to visit. The dogs? How about the fact that pups can have their very own beef taco? Get along, little doggie.

facebook.com/LittleHoppita

The Wesley Anne, Melbourne

Your pub dog might enjoy the strains of live music from an afternoon session at this one-time church on the Thornbury high street. You can park a pooch out the front but the real money is on the shady beer garden packed with mismatched furniture out the back. Jump online to check for Rover-friendly rock 'n' roll.

wesleyanne.com.au

Madame Brussels, Melbourne

Take your dog for a rooftop garden party at this veteran Melbourne bar that loves a well-behaved dog. Your pet will have to travel up in the lift to the faux-grass and lattice-filled bar where humans can have jugs of cocktails and watch the Melbourne streets below.

madamebrussels.com

Nagambie Brewery & Distillery, Strathbogie

The team behind Mitchelton Winery built this modern brewer on the banks of the Nagambie River where there is a dog-friendly deck to watch all the water sports.
facebook.com/nagambiebrewery

Western Australia

Albany Hotel, Albany

Established in 1835, the historic Albany Hotel is the oldest pub in WA's oldest town and offers a family-friendly environment with great old-fashioned pub meals. Dogs are welcome in the covered seating area at the front and back of the hotel and a water bowl is provided.
facebook.com/TheAlbanyHotelYorkStreet

Matso's Brewery, Broome

Home to the famous Matso's alcoholic ginger beer as well as a range of other brews (try the chilli-and-mango-infused beer for a real kick), Matso's aims to reflect the Asian heritage of the region and the brewery has beautiful views over Roebuck Bay. Open from 7 am till late every day of the week. Sample the extensive menu reflecting the unique and tropical flavours of Broome.
matsos.com.au

Little Creatures, Fremantle

This mammoth brewery housed in a warehouse on the water in Fremantle has tasting paddles of beer so you can sample all of the different offerings that they – one of Australia's original craft breweries – have to offer. And if you can get someone to look after your dog the brewery tours are worth a look.
littlecreatures.com.au

Who's Your Mumma?, Fremantle

From large to small, this is one of the west's first small bars and is not far from Little Creatures in Fremantle. This is the perfect spot to grab a

cocktail with your best furry bud as you watch Perth's social set in the minimalist, industrial-chic surrounds.
whosyourmumma.com.au

Margaret River Brewhouse, Margaret River
A great spot to take a break from wine tasting and head on to some beer tasting. This brewer, in a region where surf meets amazing food, produce and makers, is a great spot for dog owners to try a Red IPA, a kolsch or a pilsner. Dogs will have to stick to the water, but there is plenty of room for a stretch.
margaretriverbrewhouse.com.au

Cape Mentelle, Margaret River
This winery is only a dog walk away from the town of Margaret River itself. It's a tree-lined stroll and you can grab a cellar-door drop and head back to your stay in town. This is just one of the many dog-friendly places to try Margaret River's finest exports. See also, Lenton Brae Estate, Swings and Roundabouts, Hayshed Hill, Xanadu Wines and more.
capementelle.com.au

Greenwood Hotel, Perth
Situated to the north of the Perth CBD and not far from Sorrento Beach, this Perth pub is a great place for road-tripping rovers to stop for a drink and bite to eat.
greenwoodhotel.com.au

The Windsor Hotel, Perth
Sunday sessions in the Garden Bar are where you will find dogs of all persuasions enjoying this South Perth classic Aussie pub that first opened its doors in 1898. The bar is draped in a canopy of vines and is the perfect place for a summer afternoon.
windsorhotelsouthperth.com

CHAPTER NINE

HOTEL CITY BREAKS

Pets in the city: how upmarket hotels are chasing the doggydollar

Another area of Australian life that is catching up to the US and Europe when it comes to pup friendliness is upscale city hotels. In the US, nearly three-quarters of hotels welcome furry family members but the numbers here are much lower.

But hotels are catching on to the furry dollar given the fact that, in pre-pandemic times, Australians dropped nearly $750 million a year on spoiling their pets. Taking them on a luxury hotel staycation is the next logical step and a number of hotels are not just being pet-friendly but treating dogs, and other animals, as part of your family.

Andre Jacques, director of sales and marketing at The Langham, Melbourne oversaw one of the most recent forays into allowing pets into upmarket hotels with their Pampered Pets Staycation.

Jacques spent a lot of time while the Langham was closed during the COVID lockdown coming up with and designing new staycation packages, and with the pandemic and the increased number of pets it seemed obvious to welcome our four-legged friends to the Langham. He spent months working with the City of Melbourne council and with hotel staff. For example, any staff not comfortable with pets wouldn't be assigned to the pet-friendly rooms, so there are logistics at play as well as just popping a doggy bed into a room. There was training to consider as well as not impacting customers who do not have pets and are not interested in seeing them in hotels.

'A lot of planning and effort went into it and we are only doing it for two room types, the executive terrace and the river corner rooms,' Jacques says. 'And it has taken off very well. It is the Pampered Pet Staycations so the pets we have come to the Langham are very much the pampered types and we also wanted to cater for those people who don't have children and have pets and they spoil them and want to have them with them all the time.'

The majority of pets are dogs, but the hotel has had a few feline friends come as well. And both species are treated to a

chef-cooked in-room dining menu.

'We brought some colleagues' dogs in and did some taste testing so what appears on the menu were the most popular dishes,' he says.

The package is constantly evolving with plans for recommended groomers, sitters and new areas of the hotel for pets being looked at for the future.

This is an admittedly high-end affair but if you are looking for some serious canine indulgence then look no further than these city spots.

Adelaide

Hilton Adelaide

The Hilton is happy to have pets but there are no OTT packages as of yet, just a few house rules. Dogs must be domesticated, toilet trained and must not exceed 34 kilograms. There is one dog allowed per room and they must not be left unattended. Dogs are not permitted in public areas including food and beverage outlets, tennis court, pool or pool deck area. A $500 deposit will be held upon check-in and a $90 charge per stay is applicable in addition to the nightly room rate.
hilton.com

Brisbane

Mantra on Edward

Mantra on Edward is located within walking distance of the Roma Street Parklands and the doggy wandering available at South Bank. Pet-friendly hotel rooms are limited and are not available online, they must be booked with the property directly, so jump on the phone for a doggy stay in Brissie.

mantra.com.au

Ovolo The Valley, Fortitude Valley

The Ovolo hotels are known for whimsy and this centrally located offering is no different, with ornate suites and plenty of fun to be had. The Ovolo V.I.Pooch package welcomes canine consumers with a 'doggy bag' full of goodies as well as their own bed, bowl and bites. Like a lot of new entrants into the dog-friendly market, this chain of hotels has recognised the benefits of not just being dog-friendly but dog indulgent.

ovolohotels.com

Canberra

Mercure Canberra, Braddon

This Mercure, formerly the historic Hotel Ainslie, offers the standard Pampered Pet Package with gifts, bedding and bowls, but the hotel has also teamed up with a reputable, experienced pet-sitting service who can come to your hotel room to care for your doggy. Pet-sitting services must be booked in advance.
mercurecanberra.com.au

Abode

There are various Abode locations around Canberra and all are pet-friendly. The only catch is that not all rooms are directly accessible to an outdoor area for pet ablutions, so make sure you ask when booking to be sure you have easy access to outside.
abodehotels.com.au

Ovolo Nishi, New Acton

The Ovolo V.I.Pooch package welcomes canine consumers with a 'doggy bag' full of goodies as well as their own bed, bowl and bites.
ovolohotels.com

Quest Canberra

This mid-range hotel with two Canberra locations is pet-friendly, with doggy rooms that need an extra $200 bond refundable when you leave. If you stay longer than two weeks then the bond is automatically deducted for cleaning. It is recommended to book direct as some third-party website will book you the studios, which are not pet-friendly.
questapartments.com.au

mercure
HOTEL

Darwin

Mercure Darwin Airport Resort

Mercure Darwin Airport Resort boasts a pet-friendly bungalow, which includes pet bedding, bowls and a stuffed toy to take home. All types of household pets are welcome. For the humans, the bungalow is equipped with a semi-contained kitchenette, queen bed and private verandah. The Pampered Pet Package offers gifts, bedding and bowls but pet-friendly rooms are limited.
darwinairporthotels.com.au

Quest Palmerston

This mid-range hotel is pet-friendly with doggy rooms that need an extra $200 bond refundable when you leave. If you stay longer than two weeks then the bond is automatically deducted for cleaning. It is recommended to book direct as some third-party websites will book you the studios, which are not pet-friendly.
questapartments.com.au

Melbourne

Element by Westin, Richmond

Located in Richmond, the Element has 168 rooms but only a handful of them are pet-friendly. Rooms come with a dog bed, Bendo-branded dog bowls and a doggy mini bar with a bandana, plush toys, ball, treats and body spray. There is also a Relax Reception happy hour-and-a-half held at Mint Lane between 5 and 6.30 pm Mondays through to Thursdays with complimentary snacks.

The Langham, CBD

The Langham is the newest member of the doggy staycation club but it has made up for it with a truly indulgent offering (see introduction).
langhamhotels.com

Ovolo

The Ovolo V.I.Pooch package applies here (see Brisbane entry for details) and the new location at Ovolo South Yarra even has a secret,

80s themed bar (but doggy will have to stay behind).
ovolohotels.com

QT Melbourne

QT's package is called Pup Yeah! It offers a puppy mini bar, in-room doggy dinner menu designed by QT's 'Head of Treats' and a pupQ grooming service. The only catch is doggies need to be under 20 kilograms.
qthotels.com

Perth

Citadines, Perth

Citadines Aparthotel has jumped on the doggy bandwagon with the A PAW-fect staycation in Perth. With lush parks and dog-friendly beaches within close distance of the property, pups and their pals can explore the city. The PAW-fect staycation package includes overnight accommodation in a studio, one or two-bedroom apartment, a bed fit for the size of your furry companion, water and food bowls and 'doggy business' bags, plus a welcome pack for your PAW-fect stay including a treat, toy and a gift.
citadines.com

Quest Midland

This mid-range hotel is pet-friendly with doggy rooms that need an extra $200 bond refundable when you leave. If you stay longer than two weeks then the bond is automatically deducted for cleaning. It is recommended to book direct as some third-party websites will book you the studios which are not pet-friendly.
questapartments.com.au

Sydney

InterContinental, Double Bay

There is a pampered pooch or two in the bay so the InterContinental Double Bay offers a room ready to go with a dog bed in the lounge room and water and feed bowls in the bathroom. Should you wish to treat your

pet to in-room dining the hotel has a special pet-friendly menu that has been curated to please every pet's palate.
doublebay.intercontinental.com

The Langham Sydney
Sydney was the first Langham hotel to open its doors to dogs and offer the Pampered Pet Staycation (see introduction).
langhamhotels.com

The Old Clare, Chippendale
This boutique hotel in Chippendale offers two dog-friendly rooms but does not hold back on the spoiling. Pets will enjoy touches like a mini retro-style lounge, handmade Motion Ceramics bowls, plush toys, and complimentary in-room dining. The two options are the Kent room, perfect for a quick crash pad, or the Abercrombie if you plan to spend a bit more time lounging in the room.
theoldclarehotel.com.au

Ovolo Woolloomooloo
The Ovolo V.I.Pooch package welcomes canine consumers with a 'doggy bag' full of goodies as well as their own bed, bowl and bites.
ovolohotels.com

Pier One Sydney Harbour
This hotel offers your spoiled four-legged companions rooms with a view of Sydney Harbour. The package also offers a doggy minibar loaded with dog-friendly snacks or you can take your pup to The Gantry restaurant for a doggy degustation. Other inclusions are a doggy welcome amenity on arrival, use of premium Furf food bowl and water bowl during your stay, a luxury, eco-friendly P.L.A.Y. dog bed and direct access to the pier from your room (subject to availability).
pieronesydneyharbour.com.au

QT Sydney
The QT that kicked off the chain is right in the centre of Sydney and has the Pup Yeah package on offer (see Brisbane entry for details).
qthotels.com

INTERCONTINENTAL
HOUSE OF K'DOR
K

TRAVEL TAILS

Paul and Rafferty Chai, and Orinoco the Old English sheepdog, (@orinoco_goes) check in to The Langham Melbourne

There is something slightly surreal about taking your dog slipping and skidding across the marble floors, past ornate fountains and staff with golden trolleys full of luggage in a high-end hotel.

We have checked in to a Pampered Pet Staycation at the Langham in Melbourne, one of the most recent luxury hotels to offer such a service to pet owners who want a night of luxury with their dogs (or cats, if you prefer).

My son Rafferty and I are taking Orinoco the Old English sheepdog for a night out in Melbourne and he has been freshly washed and blow-dried by the groomer, so he is ready for this night on the town. Orinoco is just five months old and is certainly bringing the childlike enthusiasm to his new surrounds, the Executive Terrace, a corner suite with enough outdoor space to host a soiree and incredible views of the Melbourne CBD. The room is huge with floor-to-ceiling windows looking out onto the city on one side and the pool deck on the other. There is room for a couch as well. The bathroom is marble and huge, with a pair of Langham-branded pet bowls for Ori, and a plush doggy bed in the room for him to use as well.

Part of the fun of taking your pets with you anywhere is seeing them excited and interested in new surrounds and Orinoco spends ages on the balcony of The Langham, nose in the air, taking in all the new smells coming from Southbank and the CBD. He seems a little uncertain about the height at first but is soon pressing his nose up against the glass barrier for a look at the Yarra River below. Ori was less keen on the lift, where he could feel the movement but not see it, but he got used to it after a couple of trips. Sunset was spent out on the terrace, the huge amount of space meaning that we all had plenty of room, and Melbourne was turning on some great weather.

Some guests simply stay in the opulent surrounds of The Langham and order their dinner in but, with a younger dog full of energy, we called down to the concierge to see what our options were for a stroll and a bite to eat near the hotel. After checking around, he recommends the Arbory Bar & Eatery, the riverside venue right next to the famous Flinders Street Station that is dog-friendly with plenty of outdoor space.

But first Ori needs to be fed so we grab the pets' private-dining menu and order him some diced, cooked Australian beef fillet, mixed vegetables and braised barley. After a short wait it is delivered to our room and I have never seen him eat so fast in his entire life. Getting kibble into him after this is going to be a definite struggle, he is a hotel doggy now.

We grab the lead and head off over the Evan Walker pedestrian bridge to Arbory, where we order a tiki cocktail for me, a Pepsi for my son, and we keep Ori amused with the Prime100 chicken fillet treats that the Langham provided for him in our room. It is a thoughtful touch and they are used a lot during our stay.

After a short walk back to the hotel, we order up some room service dessert for the humans, while Orinoco falls asleep at the foot of our bed. It may well be a dog's life, but the humans are pretty spoiled on this staycation as well.

TIMOR SEA
Darwin
INDIAN OCEAN
Kununurra
Derby
Broome
Halls Creek
Port Hedland
Great Sandy Desert
Onslow
Exmouth
Lake Mackay
Lake Disappointment
Paraburdoo
Newman
Gibson Desert
Carnarvon
WESTERN AUSTRALIA
Lake Carnegie
Denham
Meekatharra
Wiluna
Kalbarri
Mount Magnet
Leinster
Great Victori
Desert
Geraldton
Morawa
Leonora
Laverton
Lake Barlee
Wongan
Jurien Bay
Nullarbor Plain
Perth
Northam
Merredin
Madura
Mandurah
Kondinin
Norseman
Bunbury
Ravensthorpe
Cape Naturaliste
Cape Arid
Augusta
Manjimup
Esperance
Albany
Cape Leeuwin
Great Australian B

AFURA SEA
Torres Strait
Bamaga
Weipa
Gulf of Carpentaria
Coen
CORAL SEA
Cooktown
Great Barrier Reef
Cairns
Innisfail
Normanton
Townsville
Ayr
nnant Creek
Cloncurry
Mount Isa
Hughenden
Mackay
venport
RTHERN
RITORY
Winton
Rockhampton
Barcaldine
Gladstone
e Springs
Emerald
QUEENSLAND
Bundaberg
Simpson Desert
Charleville
Roma
Sunshine Coast
Brisbane
Thargomindah
St. George
Gold Coast
STRALIA
Lake Eyre
Ballina
r Pedy
Tibooburra
Moree
Marree
Walgett
Bourke
Narrabri
Coffs Harbour
Lake Torrens
Lake Frome
Tamworth
Woomera
Wilcannia
Port Macquarie
Gilgandra
Lake Gairdner
Hawker
Broken Hill
Dubbo
Maitland
Port Augusta
Whyalla
Port Pirie
NEW SOUTH WALES
Bathurst
Newcastle
Orange
Sydney
Renmark
Goulburn
Wollongong
coln
Adelaide
Murray
Wodonga
CANBERRA
VICTORIA
Bendigo
Ballarat
Melbourne
Cape Howe
Mount Gambier
Portland
Geelong
Bass Strait
PACIFIC OCEAN
Marrawah
Scottsdale
Launceston
Tasmania
Strathgordon
Hobart
TASMANIA

About the Author

After years travelling the international film festival circuit from Cannes to Moscow for film industry publications like *Variety*, Paul Chai ended up turning to travel writing full-time as the editor of Tigerair's in-flight magazine, *Tiger Tales*, based in Singapore.

Since returning to Australia, he has been a freelance travel writer for the past decade for Nine's *Traveller* section and News Corp's *Escape* publication. He has stayed in lighthouses along the Gippsland coast, cage dived with great white sharks in Port Lincoln, South Australia and stuffed himself with enough food and wine working on *The Age Good Food Guide* to make his GP shake his head. Chai recently adopted an Old English Sheepdog, called Orinoco, who has opened up a whole new world of dog-related travel and he is now far more likely to find a plastic poo bag in his old jacket pockets than a film ticket stub.

First published in 2021
by New Holland Publishers
Sydney • Auckland

Level 1, 178 Fox Valley Road,
Wahroonga, NSW 2076, Australia
5/39 Woodside Ave, Northcote,
Auckland 0627, New Zealand

newhollandpublishers.com

A record of this book is held at the National Library of Australia.

ISBN 9781760794064

Group Managing Director: Fiona Schultz
Project Editor: Liz Hardy
Designer: Andrew Davies
Production Director: Arlene Gippert
Printed in China

10 9 8 7 6 5 4 3 2

Keep up with New Holland Publishers:

NewHollandPublishers

@newhollandpublishers